GREAT COMMISSION

AND SPIRIT SOUL AND BODY

LESLIE M JOHN

GREAT COMMISSION

AND SPIRIT SOUL AND BODY

LESLIE M JOHN

My mission is to proclaim the good news of our Lord Jesus Christ as revealed to me through Holy Bible and from various teachers, preachers, and commentators.

I share the truth of knowledge of God with others with good intention of bringing them to the knowledge of the living God, the God of Abraham, the God of Isaac, the God of Jacob, and the Father of our Lord Jesus Christ.

Great Commission and Spirit Soul and Body

My mission is to proclaim the Gospel of Lord Jesus Christ and not to convert anyone forcibly to Christianity. One may accept or reject any or part of my writings/teachings. No offense is meant to any individual or any religion or any organization.

All scriptures in electronic format are taken from KJV and Darby Translation by Public Domain, and

New International Version (NIV)

English Standard Version (ESV)

Description:

"And this gospel of the kingdom will be proclaimed throughout the whole world as a testimony to all nations, and then the end will come" (Matthew 24:14 ESV)

There is a tendency to quote Matthew 24:14 to either relax and say Jesus is not going to come until the "gospel of kingdom" is preached throughout the whole world as a testimony to all

Leslie M John

nations" or lay great emphasis in sending missionaries on foreign tours to proclaim the Gospel.

Some churches scramble to send out missionaries at war-footing to preach the Gospel with the misconception that they are fulfilling the "Great Commission" in order to see Jesus come quickly. However, man is not going to be successful in his fast running to preach the "gospel of the kingdom".

There is great misunderstanding that Church is the only instrument to carry the Gospel to the ends of the earth. Many take it as a challenge to go on foreign missionary trips at the risk of subjecting missionaries to unnecessary persecutions, and imprisonment. In some of the churches they send their children for missionary works to safe zones and leave for others areas prone for persecutions.

ISBN-13: 978-0-9985181-5-2

ISBN-10: 0-9985181-5-8

Table of Contents

Leslie M John

Leslie M John

Leslie M John

Great Commission and Spirit Soul and Body

PREFACE

It is not with intention to discourage any Christian from preaching the Gospel that this book is written, but to find the truth, and not lay unnecessary burden on preachers to risk their lives.

In the world where we live, there would arise many occasions when we may have to disobey Government and protest but there are always ways to get the things done in orderly way.

New Testament does not allow Christians to be disobedient to Government Laws, but encourages to obey the law of the land and pray for the rulers.

The Bible commands Christians to pray for the rulers, leaders, authorities of the land, where they live. (1 Timothy 2:1-2). If the rulers are forcing upon Christians, anti-Godly policies, then Christians need to pray for change of their hearts and minds to accommodate Christians and Christian values and their beliefs.

In the Old Testament there are quite few examples as to how some disobeyed the rulers and authorities. However, but they were done not resorting to insurrection against the erstwhile Governments, and yet in a way that pleased God.

Few examples that are quite obvious in the Old Testament that show the disobedience to the then Governments, but not as

9

insurrection against the Government. The rebellion was primarily to achieve God's purposes. They were done in a way that helps them to escape from the wrath of the rulers. Few examples are as follows:

1. The Two midwives in Egypt, who were commanded to kill all the male Jewish children quietly disobedient and allowed the children to live rather than killing them. (Exodus 1:20–21. They even gave excuse as to how they attempted to kill, and yet the children were born, and thus escaped from the wrath of the king. God was good to the midwives and the people greatly multiplied while God blessed the midwives. (Ref. Exodus 1:15-22).

    Pharaoh, then ordered all male Hebrew children to be thrown into river and spare daughters born to Hebrew women.

    However, God provided a way out for the baby Moses to escape from the wrath of the king, when mother of Moses could no longer hide the baby she "…she took for him an ark of bulrushes, and daubed it with slime and with pitch, and put the child therein; and she laid it in the flags by the river's brink. And his sister stood afar off, to wit what would be done to him". Thus, Moses was rescued (Exodus 2:3-6)

2. Rahab disobeyed the command of the king of Jericho and saved Israeli spies by faith because she knew God of Israel will prevail while king of Jericho would perish. (Joshua 2:1-7)

3. Jonathan did not hear his father king Saul's command and ate honey to refresh himself, but the king ordered his son to be killed. The people then resisted king Saul's command in orderly way and Jonathan prevailed (1 Samuel 14:45)

   "And the people said unto Saul, Shall Jonathan die, who hath wrought this great salvation in Israel? God forbid: as the LORD lives, there shall not one hair of his head fall to the ground; for he hath wrought with God this day. So the people rescued Jonathan that he died not" (1 Samuel 14:45)

4. Obadiah, a man of God, who feared the LORD greatly, saved one hundred prophets of God, even while the wicked queen Jezebel was killing God's prophets. That was his devotion to God and not rebellion against the wicked ruler Ahab and his wife Jezebel. God punished Ahab and Jezebel. (1 Kings 18:1 to 19:21)

5. The Bible commands Christians to pray for the rulers, leaders, authorities of the land, where they live. (1 Timothy 2:1-2). If the rulers are adopting anti-Godly policies, Christians need to pray for the change of their hearts and minds to accommodate Christians and their beliefs.

6. Protesting against the authorities to bring to their notice their anti-Christian attitude, even if they reject to honor Christians and their beliefs, is always helpful

7. God's commandment is to pray and seek the Lord's intervention. It is God's work, and Christians' responsibility is only to proclaim the Gospel of Jesus

Leslie M John

Christ, wherever it is feasible to do so. If it is not feasible to proclaim the Gospel of Jesus Christ in a peaceful way, it is better not to preach in those areas, rather than getting into legal problems and calling them as persecutions.

8. God never commanded Christians to go about in violent way to preach the Gospel of Jesus Christ nor did the Lord command to forcibly push the Gospel down the throats of unwilling people.

9. Pursue in non-violent way and seek for negotiations when Government adopts evil against Christians.

10. Whether it is in the Old Testament period of in the New Testament period, disobedience to Government laws that are quite contrary and that oppose God's laws, or when the Government in itself is evil or that which terrorizes its own citizens, is very much within the purview of Scriptures. In such circumstances Biblical laws with regard to obedience to God and His commands takes precedence over the Government laws, no matter what kind of persecution the children of God have to suffer. It is at this time that Lord Jesus Christ's instructions take effect. His words of instructions are:

"And fear not them which kill the body, but are not able to kill the soul: but rather fear him which is able to destroy both soul and body in hell" (Matthew 10:28)

11. If Government punishes Christians for being obedient God and His commands, it is persecution, and God

honors the sufferers of such persecution.

12. Shadrach, Meshach, Abednego, have disobeyed to bowing to idols and worshipping them. Obeisance to idols is tantamount to rejecting Jehovah, and accepting instructions that are contrary to the teaching of Jehovah, and the Son of God, who is Lord Jesus Christ.

Christians are very firmly commanded not to worship Antichrist or accept his 666 mark. Persecution is there in the world, and Christians cannot avoid it, but let no Christian voluntarily invite persecutions without understanding the Scriptures correctly.

This book is written to encourage preachers to serve the Lord with good biblical knowledge and Secular knowledge, as well. A Christian has to obey, not only the God's laws, but also the law of the Land. Bible encourages to obey the law of the Land, not preach against the law of the land. Bible says...

"Let every soul be subject unto the higher powers. For there is no power but of God: the powers that be are ordained of God. Whosoever therefore resist the power, resists the ordinance of God: and they that resist shall receive to themselves damnation" (Romans 13:1-2)

"I exhort therefore, that, first of all, supplications, prayers, intercessions, and giving of thanks, be made for all men; For kings, and for all that are in authority; that we may lead a quiet

13

Leslie M John

and peaceable life in all godliness and honesty. For this is good and acceptable in the sight of God our Saviour" (1 Timothy 2:1-3)

There is great danger in not understanding the truth and falling prey to persecution. The law of the land must be obeyed. God never said to go and preach against the law of the land. It is God's work, and He knows how to carry out His work.

Luke records as...

"And he said unto them, these are the words which I spoke unto you, while I was yet with you, that all things must be fulfilled, which were written in the Law of Moses, and in the prophets, and in the psalms, concerning me. Then opened he their understanding, that they might understand the scriptures, And said unto them, Thus it is written, and thus it behoved Christ to suffer, and to rise from the dead the third day: And that repentance and remission of sins should be preached in his name among all nations, beginning at Jerusalem. And ye are witnesses of these things. And, behold, I send the promise of my Father upon you: but tarry ye in the city of Jerusalem, until ye be endued with power from on high". (Luke 24:44-49)

John records as follows:

"Then said Jesus to them again, Peace be unto you: as my Father hath sent me, even so send I you. And when he had said this, he breathed on them, and saith unto them, Receive ye the Holy Ghost" (John 20:21-22)

Luke continues Lord Jesus Christ's words as follows:

"But ye shall receive power, after that the Holy Ghost is come upon you: and ye shall be witnesses unto me both in Jerusalem, and in all Judaea, and in Samaria, and unto the uttermost part of the earth. And when he had spoken these things, while they beheld, he was taken up; and a cloud received him out of their sight. (Acts 1:8-9)

Apostle Paul, after preaching to the erstwhile world in his mission trips as follows:

"For the hope which is laid up for you in heaven, whereof ye heard before in the word of the truth of the gospel; Which is come unto you, as it is in all the world; and brings forth fruit, as it doth also in you, since the day ye heard of it, and knew the grace of God in truth" (Colossians 1:5-6)

"If ye continue in the faith grounded and settled, and be not moved away from the hope of the gospel, which ye have heard, and which was preached to every creature which is under heaven; whereof I Paul am made a minister" (Colossians 1:23)

Not any major national group was left behind to hear the Gospel of the Kingdom of God, when Paul preached it, although

Leslie M John

it was true that not all the areas in the world were reached with the Gospel. The Gospel was preached, rejected and outlawed in the very first century after Jesus ascended into heaven.

Lord Jesus Christ did not make His command that He gave in Matthew 10:14-15 obsolete, when He gave Matthew 28:19-20.

"And whosoever shall not receive you, nor hear your words, when ye depart out of that house or city, shake off the dust of your feet. Verily I say unto you, it shall be more tolerable for the land of Sodom and Gomorrah in the Day of Judgment, than for that city". (Matthew 10:14-15)

"Go ye therefore, and teach all nations, baptizing them in the name of the Father, and of the Son, and of the Holy Ghost: Teaching them to observe all things whatsoever I have commanded you: and, lo, I am with you always, even unto the end of the world. Amen" (Matthew 28:19-20)

Population explosion is huge. According to Christian Encyclopedia and other sources it was estimated that by A.D. 100 there were one million Christians of about 200 million in the Roman Empire, and Christian population in 2015 was 31% of earth's 7.3 billion in 2015. At this rate can man achieve proclaiming the Gospel to everyone in the world? No! God's plans are different. Read inside this book.

Great Commission and Spirit Soul and Body

CHAPTER 1

WHAT IS GREAT COMMISSION?

The term "Great Commission" does not appear in the Bible, but just as we use few words/phrases in Christian common parlance to communicate certain meanings of the words like "Trinity", "Millennium", "Rapture", "Bema Seat of Christ", the phrase "Great Commission" is used to convey the meaning that Jesus commanded his disciples to go into the world and preach the Gospel.

ELEVEN DISCIPLES COMMISSIONED

Acts chapters 1 to 9 give us the details that the Lord gave 'great commission' before His ascension. There were eleven disciples at that time. (Judas Iscariot, the betrayer had left them, and Mathai was numbered as 12th disciple. However, Apostle Paul was the one chosen by Lord Jesus to preach the Gospel to the Gentiles. Not much is known about Mathai.

"Great Commission" is the commandment the Lord gave to His disciples, after His resurrection from the dead, and before His ascension into heaven. Great Commission is to "make disciples" of all nations. It is to preach the good news and the love of Jesus Christ baptize the believer in the name of the Father, of the Son, and of the Holy Spirit. This commission was given by

Lord Jesus Christ to His eleven disciples (one among the twelve disciples [Judas Iscariot] betrayed Jesus and left them).

JESUS SENDS OUT THE ELEVEN APOSTLES

(Later Apostle Paul was added)

"And Jesus came and said to them, All authority in heaven and on earth has been given to me. Go therefore and make disciples of all nations, baptizing them in the name of the Father and of the Son and of the Holy Spirit, teaching them to observe all that I have commanded you. And behold, I am with you always, to the end of the age." (Matthew 28:18-20 ESV)

Even before the Lord was crucified on the cross and rose from the dead, He gave commands to His disciples, and to seventy others to go and preach the Gospel of kingdom of Heaven. However, those commands were applicable to preach only to certain areas of the land in Israel, where the children of Israel lived, and not to the Gentiles.

No inference should be made that Jesus gave commands to them to preach that the unification of Northern kingdom of Israel and Southern kingdom of Israel was at hand. Jesus explicitly gave command to preach the kingdom of heaven was at hand. It should not be construed that He or His disciples preached that thousand year of reign of Jesus Christ was imminent. It was intended to preach only to the children of

Leslie M John

Israel about the kingdom of heaven/kingdom of God. In those commands Lord Jesus prohibited His disciples to go into the way of the Gentiles.

"These twelve Jesus sent out, instructing them, 'Go nowhere among the Gentiles and enter no town of the Samaritans, but go rather to the lost sheep of the house of Israel. And proclaim as you go, saying, 'The kingdom of heaven is at hand.' Heal the sick, raise the dead, and cleanse lepers, cast out demons. You received without paying; give without pay. (Matthew 10:5-8 ESV)

KINGDOM OF GOD

Important verses about "Kingdom of God"

"kingdom of God" and "kingdom of heaven" are interchangeably used in the Gospels. Matthew used the phrase saying "kingdom of heaven" whereas other Gospel writers used "kingdom of God". Lord Jesus Christ did not come into this world to establish the Davidic kingdom uniting Northern Kingdom and Southern kingdom of Israel, but to save sinners. That makes the interpretation that "kingdom of heaven" and "kingdom of God" are not separate.

Compare Matthew 11:11-12 with Luke 7:28; Matthew 13:11with Mark 4:11 and Luke 8:10; Matthew 13:24 with Mark 4:26; Matthew 13:31 with Mark 4:30 and Luke 13:18; Matthew

Great Commission and Spirit Soul and Body

13:33 with Luke 13:20; Matthew 18:3 with Mark 10:14 and Luke 18:16; and Matthew 22:2 with Luke 13:29.

In all these contexts Matthew used the phrase "kingdom of heaven" while Mark and/or Luke used "kingdom of God". Evidently, they are not separate as some interpret (one as heaven's rule during one thousand year reign of Lord Jesus Christ, and another as God's rule over everyone, every creation eternally), but they are one and the same referred to in different phrases by different Gospel writers.

The coming of kingdom of God with power is a reference to the coming of Holy Spirit during Pentecost as we read in Acts 2nd Chapter.

Matthew uses the phrase "kingdom of heaven" for e.g., "And saying, Repent ye: for the kingdom of heaven is at hand. (Matthew 3:2), "Another parable put he forth unto them, saying, the kingdom of heaven is likened unto a man which sowed good seed in his field" (Matthew 13:24) etc.

Mark uses the phrase "kingdom of God" for e.g., "Now after that John was put in prison, Jesus came into Galilee, preaching the gospel of the kingdom of God, And saying, The time is fulfilled, and the kingdom of God is at hand: repent ye, and believe the gospel". (Mark 1:14-15)

21

"And he said, whereunto shall we liken the kingdom of God? Or with what comparison shall we compare it? It is like a grain of mustard seed, which, when it is sown in the earth, is less than all the seeds that be in the earth: But when it is sown, it grows up, and becomes greater than all herbs, and shoots out great branches; so that the fowls of the air may lodge under the shadow of it" (Mark 4:30-32)

Luke uses the phrase "kingdom of God" for e.g., "But I tell you of a truth, there be some standing here, which shall not taste of death, till they see the kingdom of God" (Luke 9:27), "I tell you, Nay: but, except ye repent, ye shall all likewise perish" (Luke 13:3).

Lord Jesus sent His disciples two by two and commanded them to preach the kingdom of God as we read in Matthew 10th Chapter, Mark 6th Chapter, and Luke 9th Chapter. This was not to preach the thousand year reign of Jesus Christ, but of the kingdom of God. It was their preliminary preaching, just as if they were under training.

"And they went out, and preached that men should repent. And they cast out many devils, and anointed with oil many that were sick, and healed them" (Mark 6:12-13)

The disciples of Lord Jesus Christ preached the Gospel of Jesus Christ only after they were empowered to speak with the power of Holy Spirit (Acts 1:4 & 8). Later, Apostle Paul was chosen to preach the Gospel to Gentiles. Paul's ministry was basically intended for Gentiles, but the commission he received did not restrict him preaching to Jews in the beginning. In fact, he preached to Jews and when they rejected him he went with message of salvation to Gentiles. This does not mean the Church came into existence after Acts 28:28.

"But the Lord said unto him, Go thy way: for he is a chosen vessel unto me, to bear my name before the Gentiles, and kings, and the children of Israel" (Acts 9:15)

The commission that the Lord gave to His disciples after His resurrection was for them to go into the world and preach the Gospel of Jesus Christ

GOSPEL OF JESUS CHRIST IS THAT HE IS THE LORD, AND HE WAS RAISED FROM THE DEAD ON THE THIRD DAY OF HIS CRUCIFIXION. THE LORD COMMANDED TO PEACH THIS GOSPEL.

"Beloved, believe not every spirit, but try the spirits whether they are of God: because many false prophets are gone out into the world. Hereby know ye the Spirit of God: Every spirit that confesses that Jesus Christ is come in the flesh is of God: And every spirit that confesses not that Jesus Christ is come in the flesh is not of God: and this is that spirit of antichrist, whereof

23

ye have heard that it should come; and even now already is it in the world" (1 John 4:1-3)

Bible speaks of Gospel, which is the good news of the Lord Jesus Christ's bearing sin of mankind, His resurrection and ascension.

WHAT IS NOT GREAT COMMISSION?

It is not feeding the hungry, clothing the naked, or building homes for the poor, caring for the sick, providing civic amenities in rural areas.

It is not to become politically and socially active. It is also not to make efforts to change the world, or change society, converting individuals luring them with material things, and it is not even running orphanages.

Helping the poor is incidental to the preaching, and rendered out of love; not as essentials. Often Christians are accused of forcible conversions when they help poor out of love and concern. Many times social amenities are provided to the poor are out of love and care. Lord Jesus Christ, who declared that all power is given to Him, gave a command to His disciples to go into the world and teach people and make disciples of all nations, baptizing them in the name of the Father, of the Son, and of the Holy Spirit.

"And Jesus came and said to them, 'All authority in heaven and on earth has been given to me. Go therefore and make disciples of all nations, baptizing them in the name of the Father and of the Son and of the Holy Spirit, teaching them to observe all that I have commanded you. And behold, I am with you always, to the end of the age.'" (Matthew 28:18-20 ESV)

EMPOWERMENT OF HOLY SPIRIT

The disciples of Lord Jesus Christ preached the Gospel of Jesus Christ only after they were empowered to speak with the power of Holy Spirit (Acts 1:4 & 8). They waited at Jerusalem, as the Lord commanded them until the Holy Spirit came upon them. It was on Pentecost (50th day after resurrection of Jesus Christ) that they received the Holy Spirit, who came to be in the world to convict the world of sin, to assure the believers of their righteousness, and the world, of coming Judgment. After receiving the power to preach, the disciples preached the Gospel of Jesus Christ with authority, with the oversight and the power the Lord gave them in Matthew 28:18-20.

The signs, which were incidental to the preaching, continued as Peter and John preached and healed the sick. Similarly, Paul preached and healed the sick until the entire period of Acts of Apostles, and to the entire period running concurrent to the events in the New Testament Period until the Canonization of the Scriptures was completed. Such miraculous healings, casting away evil spirits, and signs were incidental to the preaching, manifest and observed as evidence of the power of God. Such

25

miracles are not evident in this period because God is working among people in different ways.

"For since the message declared by angels proved to be reliable, and every transgression or disobedience received a just retribution, how shall we escape if we neglect such a great salvation? It was declared at first by the Lord, and it was attested to us by those who heard, while God also bore witness by signs and wonders and various miracles and by gifts of the Holy Spirit distributed according to his will" (Hebrews 2:2-4 ESV)

THE GOSPEL

1. The Gospel of the 'KINGDOM OF HEAVEN/GOD' that deals with the fulfillment of Davidic covenant that the 'kingdom shall be established for ever before thee: thy throne shall be established forever'. (2 Samuel 7:16). This Kingdom of God includes the thousand year literal reign of Lord Jesus Christ from the throne of David in Jerusalem, as detailed in Zechariah 14:9 "And the LORD shall be king over all the earth: in that day shall there be one LORD, and his name one"

2. The "GOSPEL OF JESUS CHRIST" deals with the Salvation of mankind that Apostle Paul spoke of, as the 'Grace of God'. It is to proclaim that Jesus is Lord. He died for our sins, and that He was raised from the dead on the third day. Jesus died and was

raised for our justification and we are justified because of our belief in Him.

"For we stretch not ourselves beyond our measure, as though we reached not unto you: for we are come as far as to you also in preaching the gospel of Christ" (2 Corinthians 10:14)

3. The 'Gospel' that is called "EVERLASTING GOSPEL", preached unto those, who did not believe in him, and who will pass through the "Great Tribulation". It includes mainly Jews, and left behind Gentiles as well. It will last until every knee shall bow at the feet of Lord Jesus Christ.

"I said to him, 'Sir, you know.' And he said to me, "These are the ones coming out of the great tribulation. They have washed their robes and made them white in the blood of the Lamb" (Revelation 7:14 ESV).

4. The Gospel that is called 'ANOTHER GOSPEL', which is the perversion of the Gospel of Christ. Christians are warned to be careful about this 'another gospel' by the agents of Satan, who transforms himself as the angel of light. Apostle Paul writes about this gospel.

"I marvel that ye are so soon removed from him that called you into the grace of Christ unto another gospel: Which is not another; but there be some that trouble you, and would pervert the gospel of Christ". (Galatians 1:6-7).

Leslie M John

False apostles calling themselves as apostles of Christ preach this gospel perverting the truth of the real gospel of Jesus that Apostle Paul calls as 'my gospel' in Romans 2:16, the gospel of Christ. However, "my gospel" is not to be understood as Paul's personal Gospel, but it is the same Gospel which Peter and others preached; that is of Lord Jesus Christ's death, burial and resurrection. Paul was contradicting those who were Judaizers, who insisted on circumcision for Gentiles to be saved.

This 'another gospel' dispels the efficacy of the blood of Jesus Christ and gives importance to law and works associated with it. This gospel seeks to add works to faith in Christ. It shows that mere faith in Jesus is not enough to be saved but good works need to be done. While good works follow salvation, they are not conditional for receiving salvation.

Paul writes to the Church in Thessalonica that when they received the word of God, which they heard it from him, they received it not as the word of men, but as the truth from the word of God. He says that the truth of the Gospel will lead them to repent of their sins and help them to believe in Jesus Christ. (1 Thessalonians 2:13)

ARE WE HOLDING UP JESUS FROM COMING?

"And this gospel of the kingdom will be proclaimed throughout the whole world as a testimony to all nations, and then the end will come" (Matthew 24:14 ESV)

There is a tendency to quote Matthew 24:14 to either relax and say Jesus is not going to come until the "gospel of kingdom" is preached throughout the whole world as a testimony to all nations" or lay great emphasis in sending missionaries on foreign tours to proclaim the Gospel.

Some churches scramble to send out missionaries at war-footing to preach the Gospel with the misconception that they are fulfilling the "Great Commission" in order to see Jesus come quickly. However, man is not going to be successful in his fast running to preach the "gospel of the kingdom".

There is great misunderstanding that Church is the only instrument to carry the Gospel to the ends of the earth. Many take it as a challenge to go on foreign missionary trips at the risk of subjecting missionaries to unnecessary persecutions, and imprisonment. In some of the churches they send their children for missionary works to safe zones, and leave for others areas prone for persecutions.

That is not what Lord Jesus said in any of the four Gospels in the Bible. Revelation Chapter 14:6, 7, 9 and 11 show that God has a

29

plan to send "angel flying directly overhead, with an eternal gospel to proclaim to those who dwell on earth, to every nation and tribe and language and people"

"Then I saw another angel flying directly overhead, with an eternal gospel to proclaim to those who dwell on earth, to every nation and tribe and language and people. 7 And he said with a loud voice, 'Fear God and give him glory, because the hour of his judgment has come, and worship him who made heaven and earth, the sea and the springs of water.'" (Revelation 14:6, 7 ESV)

Apostle Paul declared in his epistles that the word of God was preached to the world (Ref. Colossians chapter 1:5-6, and 23). God uses various methods to get His word proclaimed among the nations and reach out to every individual.

Apostle Paul was chosen to preach the Gospel to Gentiles. Paul's ministry was basically intended for Gentiles, but the commission he received did not restrict him preaching to Jews in the beginning. In fact, he preached to Jews and when they rejected him he went with message of salvation to Gentiles. God uses several methods to proclaim His message before the end comes. Lord Jesus Christ would come anytime now, because the Gospel of Jesus Christ is already taken to the world.

"But the day of the Lord will come as a thief in the night; in the which the heavens shall pass away with a great noise, and the elements shall melt with fervent heat, the earth also and the works that are therein shall be burned up" (2 Peter 3:10)

THE METHODS OF REACHING OUT

1. LORD JESUS CHRIST Himself preached the Gospel

2. The Lord gave some, Apostles, some, Prophets, some, Evangelists, some, Pastors and some, Teachers For the edification of the Church (Ephesians 4:11)

3. 144 THOUSAND PREACH GOSPEL — they are sealed out of 12 Tribes of Israel. This happens after the church is "caught up" ... Revelation 7:4-8

4. THE TWO WITNESSES PREACH GOSPEL — Revelation 11:3

And I will give power unto my two witnesses, and they shall prophesy a thousand two hundred and threescore days, clothed in sackcloth. (Revelation 11:3)

5. THE ANGEL PROCLAIMS GOSPEL ... And I saw another angel fly in the midst of heaven, having the everlasting gospel to preach unto them that dwell on the earth, and to every nation, and kindred, and tongue, and people, (Revelation 14:6)

Paul declared in his epistles that the word of God was preached to the world (Ref. Colossians chapter 1:5-6, and 23). Apostle

Paul was chosen to preach the Gospel to Gentiles. Paul's ministry was basically intended for Gentiles, but the commission he received did not restrict him preaching to Jews in the beginning. In fact, he preached to Jews and when they rejected him he went with message of salvation to Gentiles.

"But the Lord said unto him, Go thy way: for he is a chosen vessel unto me, to bear my name before the Gentiles, and kings, and the children of Israel" (Acts 9:15).

The salvation of God was sent unto the Gentiles is gone out to the Gentiles.

THE WORLD

The English word "World" has several definitions. It generally is "the earth or a part of it, with its inhabitants, affairs, etc., during a particular period" or "the earth, together with all its countries, peoples, and natural features". However, biblically speaking several variant Greek words were used in the oldest manuscripts to give variant definitions. Because English word "world" is used in the Bible as a common term for variant Greek words, it is hard for common man to know the real meaning associated with the Greek words used in Scriptures in their context, and the intention behind using different Greek words that were translated as "world".

Great Commission and Spirit Soul and Body

The common occurrences of the word "world" in the New Testament are mainly from Greek definition# 2889. kosmos, (used to indicate the world, in a wide or narrow sense, including its inhabitants as in John 3:16, 17, 19), 165.aion (used to indicate an age as in Matt.28:20), 3625. oikoumene (used to indicate Roman Empire as in Matt 24:14; Luke 2:1; Luke 4:5; Luke 21:26; Acts 11:28 etc.).

Greek words are shown in brackets in the following verses from Matthew 24

And [kai] this [touto] gospel [euaggelion] of the kingdom [basileia] shall be preached [kerusso] in [en] all [holos] the world [oikoumene] for [eis] a witness [marturion] unto all [pas] nations [ethnos]; and [kai] then [tote] shall the end [telos] come [heko]. (Matthew 24:14)

Greek words are shown in brackets in the following verses from Matthew 28

And [kai] Jesus [Iesous] came [proserchomai] and spake [laleo] unto them [autos], saying [lego], All [pas] power [exousia] is given [didomi] unto me [moi] in [en] heaven [ouranos] and [kai] in [epi] earth [ge]. Go ye [poreuomai] therefore [oun], and teach [matheteuo] all [pas] nations [ethnos], baptizing [baptizo] them [autos] in [eis] the name [onoma] of the Father [pater], and [kai] of the Son [huios], and [kai] of the Holy [hagios] Ghost

33

[pneuma]: Teaching [didasko] them [autos] to observe [tereo] all things [pas] whatsoever [hosos] I have commanded [entellomai] you [humin]: and [kai], lo [idou], I [ego] am [eimi] with [meta] you [humon] alway [pas] [hemera], even unto [heos] the end [sunteleia] of the world [aion]. Amen [amen]. (Matthew 28:18-20)

MATTHEW 28: 18-20 These were the exact words spoken by Lord Jesus Christ as recorded in "Codex Sinaiticus", which is the earliest Greek manuscript.

vs. 18 And Jesus came and spoke to them, saying: All authority in heaven and on earth has been given to me.

vs. 19 Go, make disciples of all nations, baptizing them into the name of the Father and of the Son and of the Holy Spirit.

vs. 20 teaching them to observe all things whatever I commanded you. And lo, I am with you, all the days, to the conclusion of the age.

This is how these three verses were translated into King James Version.

vs. 18 And Jesus came and spake unto them, saying, All power is given unto me in heaven and in earth.

vs. 19 Go ye therefore, and teach all nations, baptizing them in the name of the Father, and of the Son, and of the Holy Ghost:

vs. 20 teaching them to, observe all things whatsoever I have commanded you: and, lo, I am with you always, even unto the end of the world. Amen. (Matthew 28:18-20 KJV)

Mark records the "Great Commission" as follows:

"And he said unto them, Go ye into all the world, and preach the gospel to every creature. He that believeth and is baptized shall be saved; but he that believeth not shall be damned" (Mark 16:15-16 KJV)

(The availability of Mark 16:9-20 in the earliest Greek Manuscripts, "Codex Sinaiticus" and Codex Vaticanus" is debatable).

THE CONTRAST

Earlier, as seen in Matthew 10, Mark 6, Luke 9 Jesus sent His disciples, two by two to preach to repent because the kingdom of heaven is at hand, and as seen in Luke 10 the Lord sent seventy, two by two, to reap the harvest. These commissions to preach the Gospel of kingdom of heaven/God were given before His crucifixion, burial and ascension for the benefit of local people in Judah, Israel. It was not meant for the world. Jesus prohibited His disciples to go in the way of Gentiles.

The command found in Mark 16:15-20 is as follows:

"And he said unto them, Go ye into all the world, and preach the gospel to every creature. He that believeth and is baptized shall be saved; but he that believeth not shall be damned. And these signs shall follow them that believe; in my name shall they cast out devils; they shall speak with new tongues; they shall take up serpents; and if they drink any deadly thing, it shall not hurt them; they shall lay hands on the sick, and they shall recover. So then after the Lord had spoken unto them, he was received up into heaven, and sat on the right hand of God. And they went forth, and preached everywhere, the Lord working with them, and confirming the word with signs following. Amen" (Mark 16:15-20)

The oldest manuscripts namely, the 'Codex Sinaiticus', and 'Codex Vaticanus' do not have Mark 16:9-20. They stop at verse 8, which is an abrupt end. There is considerable debate about ending Mark 16 and verse 8. There are people who say the rest of the portion (Mark 16:9-20) was added by the scribes to make it appear similar to the commission given in Matthew 28:19-20.

Mark 16 from Codex Sinaiticus is as follows.

1 And when the Sabbath had passed, Mary Magdalene and Mary the mother of James, and Salome bought spices, that they might come and anoint him.

Great Commission and Spirit Soul and Body

2 And very early on the first of the week they came to the sepulcher, the sun having risen.

3 And they said among themselves: Who shall roll away for us the stone from the door of the sepulcher?

4 And looking up they see that the stone had been rolled away; for it was very great.

5 And they entered the sepulcher and saw a young man, sitting at the right side, clothed in a white robe; and they were amazed.

6 But he says to them: Be not amazed. You seek Jesus the Nazarene who was crucified; he has risen, he is not here: see the place where they laid him.

7 But go, tell his disciples, especially Peter, that he goes before you into Galilee: there you shall see him, as he said to you.

8 And going out they fled from the sepulcher; for trembling and astonishment had seized them; and they said nothing to anyone, for they were afraid.

It has the following note attached to it.

[Note: According to Tischendorf, the remaining twelve verses were not written by Mark.

Codex Sinaiticus and Vaticanus have them not.

Leslie M John

The learned reader can see the proof as given by Tischendorf. See, also, Tregelles and Alford.

Codex Sinaiticus: H. L. Anderson New Testament 99]

Early Church Fathers of fourth century, namely, Eusebius and Jerome affirmed that many Greek manuscripts, which they saw, did not contain verses 9-20 of Mark. Some dispute saying Jerome discussed about versus 14 in his work "Against the Pelagians" [Pope, Kyle. "Is Mark 16:9-20 Inspired?" Biblical Insights 9.8 (August 2009): 22-2]

New Kings James Version and many other translations have Mark 16:9-20. Indeed these verses are very confusing to many believers, who interpret differently. Many have risked their lives to the point of death. There is much reason to believe that Mark picked up facts from different passages in other Gospels, to conclude his Gospel to include verses 9 to 20.

There are some evidences observed in the New Testament that give credence to the inclusion of versus 9-20 in Mark 16. Some observations are such as the devil tried to tempt Jesus by quoting Scriptures, and Jesus gaining victory over temptations by quoting Scriptures in return that rebuke the devil.

Another one is when Apostle Paul was warming up at the fire after shipwreck and landing thereafter on an island named Melita (Malta) a viper caught his hand and hung to it. The people, who tried to help him warm at the fire, said that Paul was from devil, but as soon as he shook it off, they said he was from God.

The observations mentioned in Mark 16:15-20 are practically seen on different occasions, giving it a benefit of doubt that the writer included in Mark 16:9-20, miracles done on different occasions as observations that follow the belief as a result of proclamation of the Gospel. Mark surely witnessed miracles even before the commission given by Lord Jesus Christ to go into the world and preach the Gospel.

"And they went out, and preached that men should repent. And they cast out many devils, and anointed with oil many that were sick, and healed them" (Mark 6:12-13)

The central theme of preaching the Gospel of Jesus Christ is, however, there in Mark 16:15 which reads...

"And he said unto them, Go ye into all the world, and preach the gospel to every creature" (Mark 16:15)

Jews desired to see signs. The command that was given Mark 16:15-20 was in order to fulfill the desire of Jews, who saw the signs that followed after the preaching. The things that were mentioned in this passage were not commands, but observations. It reads...

Leslie M John

"These signs shall follow them that believe.

The signs that shall followed them after they have believed were that they cast out devils, they spoke new tongues (which are languages), they took up serpents, and if they drank any deadly thing, it did not hurt them, they laid hands on the sick, who recovered. All these have come to pass and were fulfilled in the first century. Such signs are no more available.

The Lord even went up to saying...
"Give not that which is holy unto the dogs, neither cast ye your pearls before swine, lest they trample them under their feet, and turn again and rend you" (Matthew 7:6)

There is responsibility on the part of man also to seek God and find who the creator is, and how this universe and whole creation has come into existence. Science is yet to prove its theories about creation or evolution.

OUR RESPONSIBILITY

It does not absolve Christians of their responsibility of proclaiming the goodness of Lord Jesus Christ and His sacrifice for mankind. God has given us responsibility to preach His goodness and love towards mankind that they may not perish but have everlasting life. Apostle Paul writes...

"For though I preach the gospel, I have nothing to glory of: for necessity is laid upon me; yea, woe is unto me, if I preach not the gospel! For if I do this thing willingly, I have a reward: but if against my will, a dispensation of the gospel is committed unto me" (1 Corinthians 9:16-17)

"What is my reward then? Verily that, when I preach the gospel, I may make the gospel of Christ without charge, that I abuse not my power in the gospel" (1 Corinthians 9:18)

"And unto the Jews I became as a Jew, that I might gain the Jews; to them that are under the law, as under the law, that I might gain them that are under the law" (1 Corinthians 9:20)

"To the weak became I as weak, that I might gain the weak: I am made all things to all men that I might by all means save some. And this I do for the gospel's sake, that I might be partaker thereof with you" (1 Corinthians 9:22-23)

Open air preaching is restricted now-a-days. There are evidences in the Bible that some stalwarts preached God's message openly on streets. They were Noah, Jonah, Ezra, John the Baptist, Simon Peter, Apostle Paul etc. Lord Jesus Christ Himself preached "Sermon on the mount" openly.

The Lord said...

"And fear not them which kill the body, but are not able to kill the soul: but rather fear him which is able to destroy both soul and body in hell" (Matthew 10:28)

41

Haters of Christianity cannot "destroy both soul and body in hell". It is only the Lord who has control over our souls.

"Behold, I send you forth as sheep in the midst of wolves: be ye therefore wise as serpents, and harmless as doves" (Matthew 10:16)

Our final citizenship is in heaven, no doubt about it; but as long as we are on this earth we are under the laws of the land, as well.

"Blessed are they which are persecuted for righteousness' sake: for theirs is the kingdom of heaven" (Matthew 5:10)

However, those words do not permit preachers to violate the local Government laws and invite persecution voluntarily. Every preacher should know not only the national laws related to preaching but also local laws of their constituencies. Bible does not permit to violate Government laws.

Paul exhorted to obey the Law of the land. He says...

"Let every soul be subject unto the higher powers. For there is no power but of God: the powers that be are ordained of God. Whosoever therefore resists the power, resists the ordinance of God: and they that resist shall receive to themselves damnation. For rulers are not a terror to good works, but to the evil. Wilt thou then not be afraid of the power? Do that which is good, and thou shalt have praise of the same" (Romans 13:1-3)

While we preach Gospel of Jesus Christ to the people we should also bear in mind that we have to obey the law of the land.

"I exhort therefore, that, first of all, supplications, prayers, intercessions, and giving of thanks, be made for all men; For kings, and for all that are in authority; that we may lead a quiet and peaceable life in all godliness and honesty. For this is good and acceptable in the sight of God our Saviour" (1 Timothy 2:1-3)

CHAPTER 2

PETER THE FIRST ONE

Simon Peter, the disciple of Lord Jesus Christ, was the first one to preach the Gospel of Jesus Christ, after the Lord had risen from the dead.

When Peter spoke of Jesus of Nazareth that He was a man approved of God, he had full knowledge of Jesus, because Peter was a disciple of Jesus Christ. Peter knew that Mary was the earthly mother of Jesus and Joseph had purposed earlier to put her off when Joseph came to know that Mary was pregnant. Jesus was born of the Virgin Mary of the Holy Spirit (Matthew 1:20).

Later in his life Peter wrote in his 1 epistle Chapter 1 a great message honoring "God the Father of our Lord Jesus Christ, who has begotten us unto a lively hope by the resurrection of Jesus Christ from the dead to an inheritance, and undefiled, and that fades not, which is reserved for us". (1 Peter 1:3-5)

This Peter, an Apostle of Jesus Christ said in Acts 2:21-24 that whosoever shall call on the name of the Lord shall be saved. This Peter addressed the men in Israel and testified about Jesus of Nazareth that he was approved of God and did miracles and wonders and signs. Peter said that they took Jesus, who was delivered by the determinate counsel of foreknowledge of God, and killed him and that God raised Him from the pains of death, which could not hold him Jesus ascended into heaven and seated on the right hand of the Father and will come back after all his enemies are brought to His footstool. (Acts 2:21-25, 31, Psalm 16:8-11). Peter also quoted the David and his prophecy about Jesus Christ. (Psalm 110:1)

Before Peter went to meet Cornelius, an uncircumcised Gentile, a devout man, who feared God and gave much alms, and also prayed to God always, God taught a lesson to Peter. It was when Peter was still thinking about Mosaic Law and ordinances. Even though he was hungry he had determination not to eat that which was forbidden under Mosaic Law and Ordinances.

Jesus had already ascended into heaven by this time, and the Apostles had already begun preaching the Gospel of grace. It was not the kingdom message that they were preaching, but the Gospel of Grace. The message was that Jesus was crucified by sinful people like me, and that he died for saving the sinner, and that he was buried and rose on the third day from the dead and after forty days ascended into heaven.

Peter was the first one to preach about this fact as we read in Acts Chapter 2. Later in Acts Chapter 9 there is narration of how Paul, who persecuted Christians, was encountered by

Leslie M John

Jesus, who said that He was the one whom Paul was persecuting. When Christians are persecuted Jesus felt that he was being persecuted.

It was this Lord Jesus Christ, the Son of God, the very God himself, who said to Peter to go to Cornelius to give him the salvation message. Before going to Cornelius, Peter saw a man named "Aeneas" sick of palsy at Lydda. Peter said to him "...Jesus Christ maketh thee whole: arise, and make thy bed. And he arose immediately" (Acts 9:34). Because of this miracle done by Peter in the name of Jesus, many turned to the Lord. Later Peter prayed and raised Tabitha (also known as Dorcas) from the dead. Many believed in the Lord.

"Then Peter, filled with the Holy Ghost, said unto them, Ye rulers of the people, and elders of Israel, If we this day be examined of the good deed done to the impotent man, by what means he is made whole; Be it known unto you all, and to all the people of Israel, that by the name of Jesus Christ of Nazareth, whom ye crucified, whom God raised from the dead, even by him doth this man stand here before you whole. This is the stone which was set at nought of you builders, which is become the head of the corner. Neither is there salvation in any other: for there is none other name under heaven given among men, whereby we must be saved" (Acts 4:8-12)

Great Commission and Spirit Soul and Body

Apostle Peter's message has vital information as to who Jesus was, who crucified Him, how He was raised from the dead, and above all an important Gospel message that there is no salvation except by Lord Jesus Christ.

Jesus is His name. He is the Christ, the Messiah the Savior of the world. He is identified on this earth as from Nazareth. He is the head corner stone on which the building stands firm, and there is no salvation in any other than Him

CHAPTER 3

APOSTLE PAUL'S TESTIMONY

"Rejoice greatly, O daughter of Zion! Shout aloud, O daughter of Jerusalem! Behold, your king is coming to you; righteous and having salvation is he, humble and mounted on a donkey, on a colt, the foal of a donkey" (Zechariah 9:9 ESV)

"Say to the daughter of Zion, 'Behold, your king is coming to you, humble, and mounted on a donkey, on a colt, the foal of a beast of burden.'" (Matthew 21:5 ESV)

Apostle Paul proclaimed the Gospel of Jesus Christ for nearly thirty years. In his visits to various cities during his missionary work, he proclaimed that Lord Jesus Christ is the Son of God.

Paul's stand for Christ angered the Jews, who subjected him to severe persecutions. Yet, Paul stood firm for the Lord and proclaimed the goodness of Lord Jesus Christ.

 Paul, in his testimony before King Agrippa said that before his conversion to Christianity he had much grudge and hatred toward Christians and their beliefs.

Therefore, he decided to do many things contrary to the name of Lord Jesus Christ of Nazareth. He had shut up many Christians in prisons with the authority that he received from the chief priests and voiced against them when they were put to death. He punished believers in synagogue and compelled them to blaspheme Christ. His hatred towards Christians was so great that he persecuted them in even in unknown cities. Moreover, he obtained letter of authority from chief priest and was going to Damascus to execute his purpose.

Paul's addressing excels anybody's expectations that even in such a great disadvantageous position as prisoner as he was, he exclaims with much emotion "At midday, O king" and then proceeds. The way he addresses is so pleasing"

"At midday, O king, I saw in the way a light from heaven, above the brightness of the sun, shining round about me and them which journeyed with me" (Acts 26:13)

Paul's addressing next is again so pleasing

"Whereupon, O king Agrippa, I was not disobedient unto the heavenly vision" (Acts 26:19)

Paul was speaking about his conversion. He narrates as to how a great light from heaven shone around midday and Paul and all those who accompanied him fell down to the ground.

Only Paul heard a voice in Hebrew tongue from heaven that questioned him "Saul, Saul why persecutest me? It is hard for you to kick against pricks" Then Paul cried out saying "Who art

Leslie M John

thou Lord?" and the voice said "I am Jesus whom thou persecutest". But the voice from Lord Jesus Christ comforted Paul.

The Lord said to Ananias that Paul was a chosen vessel to minister the word of God and be a witness for Him, of all that he has seen, and that which he would see in future. Lord Jesus Christ sent Paul specifically to carry His Gospel to the Gentiles.

Paul said to King Agrippa that he was not disobedient to the vision and command that he received from heaven. He preached Gospel of Jesus Christ at Damascus, at Jerusalem, at Judea and Samaria and then in uttermost parts of the earth to the Gentiles.

The message he carried was that those who hear the Gospel of Jesus Christ should repent of their sins to Lord Jesus Christ and receive salvation.

It was this reason why Paul was caught by Jews in the temple and they made attempts to kill him. As he obtained command and help from God he continued preaching none other beliefs than that the prophets and Moses spoke of.

Paul spoke of prophecies that were fulfilled in Lord Jesus Christ. He preached that Christ who was spoken of by prophets needs to have come, die for the sins of mankind and be the first among the resurrected. He preached that Christ suffered death and showed light unto the Gentiles as also to the Jews.

Paul indeed realized that it is hard to kick against the pricks!

CHAPTER 4

APOSTLE PAUL'S BOLDNESS

Saul accepted Jesus as his Lord and after his conversion he was known as Paul. He became a great Apostle and served God. He was basically a Minister to the Gentiles of the Gospel of Jesus Christ. Saul's conversion was interesting.

Saul was persecuting the followers of Lord Jesus Christ by threatening with slaughter. He obtained letters from High Priest and while he was on his way to Damascus suddenly a light shone round about him and it was light from heaven. Saul fell to the ground and heard a voice, "Saul, Saul, why persecutest thou me?" Saul said, "Who art thou, Lord? And the Lord said, I am Jesus whom thou persecutest: it is hard for thee to kick against the pricks" (Acts 9:5)

Saul humbled himself and asked the Lord as to what the Lord wanted him to do. The Lord said to him to go to the city where He would show what he has to do.

Men who accompanied heard the voice but did not see any one and they were surprised. Saul rose up from the ground and could not see any one. Those who accompanied him led him by the hand to Damascus. Ananias, a disciple of Jesus, went to Saul with great reluctance; yet obeying the instructions of the Lord and prayed for him, calling him Brother Saul. After that Saul received sight and was filled with Holy Spirit and immediately he started preaching that Jesus Christ was the Son of God.

Psalmist writes in Psalm Chapter 2:1 "Why do the heathen rage, and the people imagine a vain thing?" This was a prophecy about Lord Jesus Christ who is the Son of God.

Paul writes: "What shall we then say to these things? If God be for us, who can be against us?" (Romans 8:31)

Who can stand against God and the children of God? It appears outwardly that people are persecuting the children of God but it is impossible to do so without touching the apple of the eye of God himself.

When people persecute the servants of God, it is tantamount to touching the apple of the eye of God. Without God's knowledge no one can do anything to the child of God. People who persecute the children of God will surely reap consequences of their actions. But they children of God who face persecutions will have their rewards.

Stephen knew about the heavenly rewards for him. He looked up into heaven and while giving up the spirit he cried to the Lord to forgive those who were hurting him. Jesus himself said on the cross that those who were crucifying him did not know what they were doing and, therefore, he cried to the Father to forgive them.

Saul could neither persecute any one; nor was the persecution launched against him for standing for Christ was successful. Paul faced illegal charges and was imprisoned; yet he faced and defended himself with great courage. God was with him always.

The Jews heard Saul preach in the very beginning days of his conversion that Jesus is the Son of God and Jesus is the very Christ. Unable to tolerate his preaching the Jews took counsel to kill him. This was the beginning of Paul's own persecution and for living for Christ.

It is evident from Chapters 21 to 28 of the Book of Acts that Apostle Paul was by nature a very bold man and faced persecutions and accusations with great courage.

"Thrice was I beaten with rods, once was I stoned, thrice I suffered shipwreck, a night and a day I have been in the deep". 2 Corinthians 11:25

Agabus, a prophet during his days prophesied against Paul that he will be arrested by the Jews and will be given over to the Gentiles, but he never got discouraged. He was falsely alleged and was put in prison. Paul boldly defended himself. Paul faced shipwrecks but was never discouraged. He encouraged others.

Great Commission and Spirit Soul and Body

Great Commission and Spirit Soul and Body

He wrote to Timothy, whom he considered as his son in the Lord,

"Holding faith, and a good conscience; which some having put away concerning faith have made shipwreck": (1 Timothy 1:19)

In 2 Corinthians 12th Chapter Paul wrote that he had weakness, which is not clearly revealed to us. He prayed to God three times to take away that weakness, but God said to him that in Paul's weakness was God's strength.

"And he said unto me, My grace is sufficient for thee: for my strength is made perfect in weakness. Most gladly therefore will I rather glory in my infirmities, that the power of Christ may rest upon me". (2 Corinthians 12:9)

Leslie M John

CHAPTER 5

SPIRIT SOUL AND BODY

(The explanation is biblical and in context of 1 Thessalonians 5:23 — not for argument or debate with unsaved people)

The order is Spirit, Soul and Body, but for the sake of convenience we explain 'body' first, then 'soul' and then 'Spirit'.

BODY

It is the external structure of man-made of dust by God. It is accessed through five senses of man... 1. Touch 2. hear, 3. See, 4. Taste and 5. Smell

Our bodies are made of dust and will return to dust. When Lord Jesus returns the body of believer is redeemed and is raised as glorified body.

"Jesus answered and said unto him, Verily, verily, I say unto thee, Except a man be born again, he cannot see the kingdom of God. Nicodemus saith unto him, How can a man be born when he is old? can he enter the second time into his mother's womb, and be born? Jesus answered, Verily, verily, I say unto thee, Except a man be born of water and of the Spirit, he cannot enter into the kingdom of God. That which is born of the flesh is flesh; and that which is born of the Spirit is spirit" (John 3:3-6)

Great Commission and Spirit Soul and Body

Born-again child of God is born of the Spirit; born from above. "Born of water" denotes water-breaking during child's birth and entrance of the child into this world. This is physical birth. Some people believe that "water" in the phrase "born of water" denotes the Word of God; but it can hardly be substantiated with Scriptures.

Lord Jesus said man should be born of water and of the Spirit to enter the kingdom of God to be with Him forever and ever (In fact, the scripture says man cannot see the kingdom of God, if he not born-again).

There are only two ways – either receive everlasting life or receive everlasting damnation in the 'lake of fire'; there is no midway! All those who are born-again will have everlasting life, and others will be damned to 'lake of fire' as the Scripture says in Revelation 20:10.

Lord Jesus Christ is inviting everyone, who is not saved yet, to confess sins to Him, acknowledge Him as the Lord, and believe in heart that God raised Him from the dead.

Upon receiving salvation free of cost from the Lord, the spirit of man is redeemed instantly, and the Spirit of Christ indwells him instantly. The Spirit cannot be defiled, no matter what kind of sin a believer might commit, after being saved; but wait a minute... a believer will not commit sin says Scripture! That is to

57

say, a true Christian will not commit sin; but there might arise many circumstances in the lives of born-again believers, where they are unwillingly or ignorantly commit transgression of God's laws, which constitutes as sin, in which case the pardon is always available from the Lord (cf. 1 John 1:8-10)

"For we know that the whole creation groans and travails in pain together until now. And not only they, but ourselves also, which have the first-fruits of the Spirit, even we ourselves groan within ourselves, waiting for the adoption, to wit, the redemption of our body" (Romans 8:22-23)

Some interpret that body is also redeemed based on 1 Corinthians 6:14-20 saying that our body is Temple of God.

However, other references show that our bodies are not yet redeemed, but only spirit part of our body is redeemed. 1 Corinthians 6:14-20 admonishes us to keep our body pure because it is the Temple of God. We are not supposed to defile it.

The indwelling of the Holy Spirt in each believer's body does not mean the body of believer is redeemed, but the command demands from us to keep our bodies blameless and pure. These verses also do not refer to the body of Christ, which is 'ecclesia' (Church), but refers to the body of each one of us.

Great Commission and Spirit Soul and Body

The Church is the body of Christ and He is the head of the Church. We are part of that whole body of Christ. The Church will be 'caught up' when the Lord comes again.

1 Thessalonians 4:16-17 show that when the Lord comes the dead in Christ shall rise first, and the believers who are alive at that time will be caught up together with them in the clouds in that order. That is not what 1 Corinthians 6:14-20 is referring to.

"And God hath both raised up the Lord, and will also raise up us by his own power. Know you not that your bodies are the members of Christ? Shall I then take the members of Christ, and make them the members of a harlot? God forbid. What? Know ye not that he which is joined to a harlot is one body? For two, saith he, shall be one flesh. But he that is joined unto the Lord is one spirit. Flee fornication. Every sin that a man doeth is without the body; but he that commits fornication sinneth against his own body. What? Know ye not that your body is the temple of the Holy Ghost which is in you, which ye have of God, and ye are not your own? For ye are bought with a price: therefore glorify God in your body, and in your spirit, which are God's" (1 Corinthians 6:14-20)

"For the Lord himself shall descend from heaven with a shout, with the voice of the archangel, and with the trump of God: and the dead in Christ shall rise first: Then we which are alive and

59

remain shall be caught up together with them in the clouds, to meet the Lord in the air: and so shall we ever be with the Lord" (1 Thessalonians 4:16-17)

The Spirit of God engulfs man's spirit, which is redeemed and is sealed. The admonition is that man should not allow soul and body to be unison in purpose to defeat the purpose of the Spirit. Flesh is always at war with the Spirit. (cf. Galatians 5:16-26)

"Who hath also sealed us, and given the earnest of the Spirit in our hearts" (2 Corinthians 1:22)

"Therefore if any man be in Christ, he is a new creature: old things are passed away; behold, all things are become new" (2 Corinthians 5:17)

SOUL

It is the life of man. It is the conscience and emotional part of man. It is the mind and heart of man. When God breathed His breath into the nostrils of man, man became a living soul.

The soul cannot be accessed through any of the five senses listed under body, but it can be accessed through our actions, words etc. It is the conscience of a man that pricks in heart to realize whether or not he is wrong.

Great Commission and Spirit Soul and Body

The conviction is by the conscience, and not by the Holy Spirit. The Holy Spirit convicts us of our righteousness; not of sin and not of judgment.

That is how all those who lived after Adam and Eve were thrown out from the Garden of Eden until the law was given (which was in Moses's period) lived in conscience and were judged according to their conscience. It is by conscience that the people in Noah's period, and during Sodom and Gomorrah's destruction period were judged.

A child knows stealing sugar from a bottle when mother is absent is wrong. No law required to tell the child that the child did something wrong.

If I say something that offends a person, he/she feels angry at me; likewise, if I appreciate a person he feels happy. This is how soul can be accessed.

If our soul were redeemed right now, we would live a perfect life, but it is not redeemed yet. Soul is redeemed only at the second coming of Jesus Christ. The soul is always in conflict with the Spirit.

It is by paying heed to the Spirit that a believer over comes the conflict between soul and spirit. Flesh is sinful nature of man. Carnal is being worldly and sensual. Spiritual is divine (Romans 8:5-8)

61

"For ye are yet carnal: for whereas there is among you envying, and strife, and divisions, are ye not carnal, and walk as men?" (1 Corinthians 3:3)

"So then they that are in the flesh cannot please God" (Romans 8:8)

"This I say then, Walk in the Spirit, and ye shall not fulfil the lust of the flesh. For the flesh lusts against the Spirit, and the Spirit against the flesh: and these are contrary the one to the other: so that ye cannot do the things that ye would. But if ye be led of the Spirit, ye are not under the law. Now the works of the flesh are manifest, which are these; Adultery, fornication, uncleanness, lasciviousness, Idolatry, witchcraft, hatred, variance, emulations, wrath, strife, seditions, heresies, Envying, murders, drunkenness, retellings, and such like: of the which I tell you before, as I have also told you in time past, that they which do such things shall not inherit the kingdom of God. But the fruit of the Spirit is love, joy, peace, longsuffering, gentleness, goodness, faith, Meekness, temperance: against such there is no law. And they that are Christ's have crucified the flesh with the affections and lusts. If we live in the Spirit, let us also walk in the Spirit. Let us not be desirous of vain glory, provoking one another, envying one another" (Galatians 5:16-26)

SPIRIT

By default, spirit in everyone is dead. However, when a person is born again the Spirit is made alive (ref. Ephesians 2:1).

"And you hath he quickened, who were dead in trespasses and sins" (Ephesians 2:1)

CHAPTER 6

OUR LIFE IN ETERNITY

We, the saved children of God do not look at things which are seen inasmuch as the earthly things are temporal and we are sojourners on this earth. Our hope is that we will have everlasting life and we will be with the Lord Jesus Christ forever and ever.

Therefore, we look for the things that are not seen because the things that are not seen are eternal. Our earthly house of this tabernacle gets dissolved but we have, in heaven, a building of God, the house that is not made with hands, but that which would be eternal in heavens.

No doubt, because our bodies are made of dust, we groan when diseases strike us. We seek in this body, to be clothed upon; but there will come a day, in the lives of each one of us, when we leave behind our frame made of dust, to be raised in glorified body at the second coming of Lord Jesus Christ.

It is so comforting for believers in Christ to know that God forgave us of our sins, never to remember, no matter how serious they were.

Great Commission and Spirit Soul and Body

The salvation is available for all, who confess their sins to the Lord, and acknowledge by mouth that Jesus is Lord, and believe in heart that God raised Jesus from the dead on the third day. God is loving, longsuffering and compassionate.

"Then shall the dust return to the earth as it was: and the spirit shall return unto God who gave it". (Ecclesiastes 12:7)

The deeds done in our earthly bodies will be judged by God.

"For God shall bring every work into judgment, with every secret thing, whether it be good, or whether it be evil" (Ecclesiastes 12:14)

Psalmist writes: "For he knoweth our frame; he remembers that we are dust". (Psalms 103:14)

Apostle Paul writes...

"While we look not at the things which are seen, but at the things which are not seen: for the things which are seen are temporal; but the things which are not seen are eternal" (2 Corinthians 4:18)

"For we know that if our earthly house of this tabernacle were dissolved, we have a building of God, an house not made with hands, eternal in the heavens" (2 Corinthians 5:1)

The spirit in unregenerate person is dead, and that is why, the natural man does not understand Spiritual things. That which is born of flesh is flesh, and that which is born of spirit is spirit. (cf. John 3:6)

The Spirit neither grows, nor diminishes. The Spirit also does not dwell in bits and pieces or indwell in installments. The Spirit is already redeemed in the case of born-again man. The soul and body are yet to be redeemed.

The soul and body will be redeemed when Lord Jesus comes again. Upon the death of man, the spirit, which is breath of God, breathed into the nostrils of man, returns to God.

None of us have seen our faces with our eyes, and we can see our faces only in reflection in a mirror. If a mirror is made of convex lens, or concave lens, our structure in reflection appears entirely different. That is to say that spiritual things can be accessed only through the window of the Holy Scriptures [The Bible])

John's reclining on Jesus body is good example to understand the difference between the human body and the spiritual body. When John saw the Lord in His glory as recorded in Revelation 1, he was wonderstruck.

CHAPTER 7

THE GOOD NEWS!

In this world, where we hear bad news all the time, here is the Word of God that comforts us, and it is the Good News. Lord Jesus Christ is the way, the truth and the life. This is the hope that there is after-life for us. Lord Jesus is coming again. His coming is imminent.

The Bible says we are all born sinners; and while we are dead in our trespasses, God sent His one and only Son, Lord Jesus Christ into this world that whoever believes in Him will not perish but have everlasting life. He relinquished His glory with the Father, and came down in the form of a servant and in the likeness of man to save mankind from sin, and afford everlasting life.

"In a moment, in the twinkling of an eye, at the last trump: for the trumpet shall sound, and the dead shall be raised incorruptible, and we shall be changed" (1 Corinthians 15:52)

The Bible says we are all born sinners; and while we are dead in our trespasses, God sent His one and only Son, Lord Jesus Christ into this world that whoever believes in Him will not perish but have everlasting life.

He relinquished His glory with the Father, and came down in the form of a servant and in the likeness of man to save mankind from sin, and afford everlasting life.

Jesus died upon the cross of Calvary so that we may be reconciled unto the Father. He was buried and was raised from the dead on the third day. The death could not hold him.

"God raised him up, loosing the pangs of death, because it was not possible for him to be held by it" (Acts 2:24 ESV)

All those who are saved are redeemed from their sins and have obtained forgiveness of their sins through Jesus Christ.

"But to all who did receive him, who believed in his name, he gave the right to become children of God" (John 1:12 ESV)

By offering Himself upon the cross of Calvary, Jesus opened the way for everyone to be saved. Jesus died for our sake as atonement for our sins. He was the perfect sacrifice.

The Bible says we are all born sinners; and while we are dead in our trespasses, God sent His one and only Son, Lord Jesus Christ into this world that whoever believes in Him will not perish but have everlasting life.

JESUS SAID "Except a man be born again, he cannot see the kingdom of God"

What does it mean to be born-again?

Great Commission and Spirit Soul and Body

Great Commission and Spirit Soul and Body

"Jesus answered and said unto him, Verily, verily, I say unto thee, Except a man be born again, he cannot see the kingdom of God. Nicodemus saith unto him, how can a man be born when he is old? Can he enter the second time into his mother's womb, and be born? Jesus answered, Verily, verily, I say unto thee, except a man be born of water and of the Spirit, he cannot enter into the kingdom of God". (John 3:3-5)

"for all have sinned and fall short of the glory of God" (Romans 3:23 ESV)

"For the wages of sin is death, but the free gift of God is eternal life in Christ Jesus our Lord" (Romans 6:23 ESV)

"... if you confess with your mouth that Jesus is Lord and believe in your heart that God raised him from the dead, you will be saved. 10 For with the heart one believes and is justified, and with the mouth one confesses and is saved" (Romans 10:9-10 ESV)

CHAPTER 8

CAN ONE SAVE ONESELF?

When someone insists on keeping the law in order to obtain salvation and then be counted as righteous before God, it is no doubt, tantamount to making his/she own efforts to achieve eternal life without the help from God.

As a consequence of his/her own efforts he/she tries to be perfect in all respects. It would then call for introspection to see if the person is indeed keeping all the provisions of the law that are to be kept mandatorily as laid down by God.

Introspection would bring conviction that even in keeping the law meticulously the law finds him guilty on one count or the other.

The only recourse left for man is to take refuge in the 'grace' of God given abundantly to us, through His only begotten Son Jesus Christ. As written in Romans 2 Chapter, those without the law shall perish without law, and those that have sinned in the law will become liable for judgment under the law.

Inasmuch as the law was given by God through Moses, Gentiles are reckoned as having no law, and therefore, if they try to obey the law meticulously, they are making the law unto themselves;

the law that was not given by God. They accuse and excuse one another according to their own law.

As for Jews the Scripture calls them 'blind' who guide the 'blind', a light of them who are in 'darkness', an instructor of the 'foolish', a teacher of 'babes', Scriptures asks Jews, who teach others about law, as to why they do not teach unto themselves the law and strict provision therein? If they are true to their teaching, then are they not stealing, while teaching not to steal? Why do they commit adultery?

"Neither is there salvation in any other: for there is none other name under heaven given among men, whereby we must be saved" (Acts 4:12)

"For God so loved the world that he gave his only begotten Son, that whosoever believeth in him should not perish, but have everlasting life. For God sent not his Son into the world to condemn the world; but that the world through him might be saved" (John 3:16-17)

Bible is very strict on them that they being teachers of the law, they break the law and commit idolatry, resulting in blasphemy of God among the Gentiles. Circumcision profits only if the law is kept in perfect sense, but if one of the provisions of the law is broken, circumcision is tantamount to un-circumcision.

71

Leslie M John

The punishments under law are very severe. Neither Jew nor Gentile can have redemption from their sins, if they rely on keeping the law and be justified. God invites everyone to accept 'grace' available through Jesus Christ, the only begotten Son of God and receive salvation. (Romans 2:12-29)

CHAPTER 9

EVERY KNEE SHALL BOW

"For it is written, As I live, saith the Lord, every knee shall bow to me, and every tongue shall confess to God" (Romans 14:11)

Paul quotes the scripture from the Old Testament and makes a point that everyone will stand before the LORD to be judged of one's sin and give account to the LORD GOD, the Holy One of Israel, and the Father of our Lord Jesus Christ. He is the salvation and in Him is the salvation, and there is no salvation in any other. (cf. Acts 4:12) "

And the LORD shall cause his glorious voice to be heard, and shall shew the lighting down of his arm, with the indignation of his anger, and with the flame of a devouring fire, with scattering, and tempest, and hailstones" (Isaiah 30:30)

To Israel, His children, the LORD gave rain in due season in order that the land may yield her increase and the trees of the field may yield their fruit (cf. Lev. 26:4), but to the Egyptians under Pharaoh, He gave them hail and rain, and flaming fire in their land.

In the land of Egypt, where Pharaoh was all in all, and where his pride and arrogance reached their peak, the plagues that he and his people suffered was apt. Fire ran along with hail upon the ground destroying every living creature.

The ten plagues Egyptians suffered were signs and proofs of Jehovah's outstretched arm against them and His presence in the land. The LORD redeemed His children physically from slavery when they cried unto the LORD with his mighty and outstretched arm.

God spoke to people in different periods of time in different ways. He spoke to the children of Israel by the prophets and protected them from harm by their enemies. He punished kings and mighty men of valor, who stood against His children. Yet, when the children of Israel worshipped idols He chastised them time and again.

God sent His one and only Son into this world to show His compassion and redeem all those who believe in Jesus as Lord. Jesus turned water into wine, increased five loaves and two fishes to feed multitudes of people, gave sight to the blind, brought dead Lazarus to life, and He, who knew no sin, was made sin for us, in order that we may be saved.

He suffered painful death upon the cross on behalf of us, in order that we may have everlasting life in abundance. Every knee will bow before Him one day. It is time now to accept the truth that Jesus is the way, the truth and the life, and be saved (cf. John 14:6).

Rejection of His compassion will be very costly and they will face judgment at the "great white throne" and all those whose names are not found in the "book of life" will be cast into the "lake of fire" (Cf. Rev. 20:15)

"That at the name of Jesus every knee should bow, of things in heaven, and things in earth, and things under the earth" (Philippians 2:10)

CHAPTER 10

IS BEING RICH A SIN?

For the love of money is the root of all evil: which while some coveted after, they have erred from the faith, and pierced themselves through with many sorrows. (1 Timothy 6:10)

It is imperative that we take note of the sources from where the money comes from before we conclude that all the money that we have is the root of evil. There is an important word "love" in this verse (1 Timothy 6:10) and that is the root of all the evil. "The love of money is the root of all evil".

It is also important to define the meaning of "covet" before we know the difference between the legitimate earnings, and the illegitimate earnings.

Scriptures lay much emphasis is unlawful gain of money by coveting.

"covet" means to desire wrongfully; to feel strong or immoderate desire for that which is another's. one of the important commandment of the Ten Commandments is...

"You shall not covet your neighbor's house; you shall not covet your neighbor's wife, or his male servant, or his female servant, or his ox, or his donkey, or anything that is your neighbor's." (Exodus 20:17 ESV)

James 2:10 says...

"For whoever keeps the whole law but fails in one point has become guilty of all of it" (ESV)

Most of us, in fact all of us, violate this commandment, which, then is tantamount to breaking the entire law. This is what happens in most cases, when a man tries to become rich by coveting and earning money in illegal ways.

In his first letter to Timothy, Apostle Paul emphatically says, by the commandment of God our Savior that rich will fall into temptations and into manifold foolish and hurtful lusts.

Although Timothy was not Paul's biological son, Paul loved him as his own son and eventually made him responsible to oversee a church by himself.

Of many good advises Paul gave Timothy, his grave concern was that he or his congregation may not focus on money. Foolish and hurtful lusts, he says, will sink men into destruction and perdition. He, then, conclusively says that the love of money is the root of all evil.

Those who longed for money by coveting ended up in sorrow, sickness and became victims of many vile desires. This was true

77

not only in the days of Timothy, but is true in our generation as well.

Lord Jesus said...

"For it is easier for a camel to go through the eye of a needle than for a rich person to enter the kingdom of God." (Luke 18:25 ESV)

The following is the context in which the Lord said these words (Luke 18:25)

When Peter and other disciples heard the words of Lord Jesus that it is hardly possible for a rich man to enter into the kingdom, as is impossible for a camel to go through the eye of needle, the Lord said to them because they followed the Lord on this earth, they will be blessed in eternity and will be seated upon the twelve thrones, judging the twelve tribes of Israel. Their seating will be along with the Lord, who will be on His throne in His glory.

The Lord added further saying those everyone, who forsakes his house or brothers or sisters or father, or wife or children of lands for His name 'sake, or as mentioned in Luke for the kingdom of God's sake, will receive an hundred fold on this earth, and will inherit everlasting life enter into the kingdom of God! For it is easier for a camel to go through a needle's eye, than for a rich man to enter into the kingdom of God. And they that heard it said, who then can be saved? And he said, the things which are impossible with men are possible with God. Then Peter said, Lo, we have left all, and followed thee. And he said unto them, Verily I say unto you, There is no man that hath left house, or parents, or brethren, or wife, or children, for the kingdom of God's sake, Who shall not receive manifold more in this present time, and in the world to come life everlasting". (Luke 18:18-30)

(It can also be seen in Matthew 19:27; Mark 10:25 and Luke 18:18 in their context)

The pursuit by the ruler was 'eternal life'. In reply to Jesus advice the ruler said, he kept the commandments. Then Jesus says to him to sell all that he has in order that he may have treasure in heaven. The ruler was not happy with the reply and went away. Jesus says "... it is easier for a camel to go through a needle's eye, than for a rich man to enter into the kingdom of God".

It is then that Peter had a question for Jesus. He says..."Lo, we have left all, and followed thee. And he said unto them"

Jesus replies saying..."Verily I say unto you, There is no man that hath left house, or parents, or brethren, or wife, or children, for the kingdom of God's sake, Who shall not receive manifold

Leslie M John

more in this present time, and in the world to come life everlasting".

His reply that has phrase "present time" not only was a reference to the eternal blessings, but also about the blessings on this world. We may not take literally, hundred-fold and apply it mathematically to parents, brethren, wife, and children. It was metaphor used to denote manifold blessings, such as is written by Luke in 18:30.

"Who shall not receive manifold more in this present time, and in the world to come life everlasting. (Luke 18:30)

The blessings may not be similar in the case of each believer may vary, but surely the child of God will not beg for bread. The life on this earth for a believer may include persecutions, and may not be like a bed of roses, yet he is assured...

"And the peace of God, which passes all understanding, shall keep your hearts and minds through Christ Jesus" (Philippians 4:7)

Psalmist wrote:

"I have been young, and now am old; yet have I not seen the righteous forsaken, nor his seed begging bread" (Psalms 37:25)

The context in Matthew 19:23-29; Mark 10:17-30; and Luke 18:18-30 is the same and blessings are manifold on this earth

Great Commission and Spirit Soul and Body

and in eternity. The words of Lord Jesus Christ cannot be twisted or removed from the Bible. They are as true as the Son of God Himself. All poor will not become rich of the same status, but surely the child of God will not beg for bread.

Those who longed for money by coveting ended up in sorrow, sickness and became victims of many vile desires. This was true not only in the days of Timothy, but is true in our generation as well.

On the contrary, Bible teaches that we should ask God according to His purpose. Seating will be along with the Lord, who will be on His throne in His glory. The Lord added further saying those everyone, who forsakes his house or brothers or sisters or father, or wife or children of lands for His namesake, or as mentioned in Luke for the kingdom of God's sake, will receive an hundredfold on this earth, and will inherit everlasting life.

"When his disciples heard it, they were exceedingly amazed, saying, who then can be saved? But Jesus beheld them, and said unto them, with men this is impossible; but with God all things are possible. Then answered Peter and said unto him, Behold, we have forsaken all, and followed thee; what shall we have therefore?" (Matthew 19:25-27)

Leslie M John

"But Jesus beheld them, and said unto them, with men this is impossible; but with God all things are possible" (Matthew 19:26)

Abraham was rich not only spiritually but on this earth, as well.

"And the scripture was fulfilled which saith, Abraham believed God, and it was imputed unto him for righteousness: and he was called the Friend of God" (James 2:23)

"And Abram was very rich in cattle, in silver, and in gold" (Genesis 13:2)

Isaac was rich...

"Then Isaac sowed in that land, and received in the same year a hundredfold: and the LORD blessed him. And the man waxed great, and went forward, and grew until he became very great" (Genesis 26:12-13)

Job was rich...

"His substance also was seven thousand sheep, and three thousand camels, and five hundred yoke of oxen, and five hundred she asses, and a very great household; so that this man was the greatest of all the men of the east" (Job 1:3)

Solomon was rich...

"And all the drinking vessels of king Solomon were of gold, and all the vessels of the house of the forest of Lebanon were of pure gold: none were of silver; it was not anything accounted of in the days of Solomon" (2 Chronicles 9:20)

David wrote...

"They shall not be ashamed in the evil time: and in the days of famine they shall be satisfied. (Psalms 37:19)

David was rich...

"And he died in a good old age, full of days, riches, and honor: and Solomon his son reigned in his stead" (1 Chronicles 29:28)

Joseph was rich...

"And Joseph gathered up all the money that was found in the land of Egypt, and in the land of Canaan, for the corn which they bought: and Joseph brought the money into Pharaoh's house" (Genesis 47:14)

Joseph rose to become governor in the land of Egypt.

There are many believers in Christ, who are blessed with excellent secular positions and wealth. God blessed them with riches and prosperity.

Legal earnings and rejoicing in the Lord are not wrong, but it the prosperity gospel that diverts the main salvation message that is wrong. The Holy Scriptures command us to do God's will, but the prosperity gospel teaches destructive greed and foolish lusts. Christians should clearly distinguish between what is to be sought and what not to be sought. Any kind of propaganda luring Christians to accumulate wealth in an unbiblical way is heresy and wrong.

A Christian should be careful when he hears a phrase, namely, "positive confession". It teaches that if you demand from God with your own creative power, He is obliged to fulfill your desire.

It goes to say that God's power to withhold something from you can be nullified by your positive faith. On the contrary, Bible teaches that we should ask God according to His purpose.

"And we know that all things work together for good to them that love God, to them who are the called according to his purpose" (Romans 8:28)

"And this is the confidence that we have in him, that, if we ask any thing according to his will, he heareth us" (1 John 5:14)

CHAPTER 11

THE LOVE OF GOD

"Behold, what manner of love the Father hath bestowed upon us, that we should be called the sons of God: therefore the world knoweth us not, because it knew him not" (1 John 3:1)

It is the abundant love that God bestowed upon us that we are called and made "sons of God" and when we see Him at His second coming we shall be like him as He is.

The world does not know this mystery, nor would it understand the love that God has bestowed upon us to make sons of God.

The reason is simple; it is because the world does not know the God of gods, and the Lord of lords, and the King of kings, who loved us and sent his one and only begotten Son that whosoever believes in him shall not perish but have everlasting life.

There is a responsibility given to the children of God, who loved us, and demands from us that we should lead a pure life even as he is pure. It is not that we are infallible, and our salvation will be lost if we commit sins, inadvertently, or deliberately, but the Word of God says that he, who commits sin is of the devil, because devil sinned from the beginning, and keeps tempting the children of God, to fall into sins.

Whosoever sins transgresses the law, and the transgression of the law is Sin. Whosoever abides in the Lord, and born-again does not sin, and whoever sins has not understood His love.

Apostle John exhorts that let no man deceive us about righteousness, but understand clearly that he who does righteousness is righteous, even as the Lord is righteous.

It is not because of our good works or ability to save ourselves that we are saved, but because Jesus paid price for our salvation that we are saved and his righteousness is imputed to us.

"There was a man of the Pharisees, named Nicodemus, a ruler of the Jews: The same came to Jesus by night, and said unto him, Rabbi, we know that thou art a teacher come from God: for no man can do these miracles that thou doest, except God be with him.

Jesus answered and said unto him, Verily, verily, I say unto thee, except a man be born again, he cannot see the kingdom of God. Nicodemus saith unto him, how can a man be born when he is old? Can he enter the second time into his mother's womb, and be born?

Great Commission and Spirit Soul and Body

Jesus answered, Verily, verily, I say unto thee, except a man be born of water and of the Spirit, he cannot enter into the kingdom of God. That which is born of the flesh is flesh; and that which is born of the Spirit is spirit" (John 3:1-6)

CHAPTER 12

FEET WASHING: SPIRITUAL SIGNIFICANCE

Is it not amazing to note that the creator of this universe came down into this world in the form of a servant and in the likeness of man and lived among men? He had his disciples with varied attitudes.

At a time when Lord Jesus knew that His time was up and has to leave this earth, Judas Iscariot was busy planning to betray the Lord. Other disciples were arguing within themselves as to who is greater than the other among themselves.

Bible says...

"And they began to enquire among themselves, which of them it was that should do this thing. And there was also a strife among them, which of them should be accounted the greatest" (Luke 22:23-24)

The Lord explains to His disciples that kings of this earth exercise their authority over their people, but in the spiritual realm, the Lord's kingdom would be different. He says to His disciples that he that is greatest among them, should be as younger, and he that is chief should be like one who serves (cf. Luke 22:25, 26)

Great Commission and Spirit Soul and Body

In John 13:1-17 a very distinct and notable event is seen. Just before the Lord ate Passover meal and instituted the Lord's Supper in the upper room (cf. Mark 14:13-15), Lord Jesus said He came not to be served but to serve and to give His life as ransom for many.

Walking barefoot, or with sandals on the dirty roads in Israel the disciples had surely had upon their feet enough dirt that needed to be washed away before they ate Passover meal and participated in the Lord's Supper.

It was at this last meeting with His disciples. That Lord Jesus teaches a visible example of servitude, and love. He rises and lays aside His garments, and takes a towel, girds Himself. Then, He pours water into a basin, and washes the feet of His disciples, and wipes with the towel that he girded Himself with.

Prophet Isaiah describes in prophecy how our Lord humbles Himself to serve others and lays His life for others. Here is the fulfilment of that prophecy in John 13:3-10.

In the present day situation we are not walking barefoot nor our streets are dirty that we need our priests and elders wash our feet before Lord's Supper, but there is significant spiritual lesson as to how we, the Lord's people as we are, should behave before the Lord's supper and thereafter in everyday life.

Leslie M John

The Lord taught a great lesson here that it is not ritual that is important but it is the heart and attitude of the believer that matters.

CHAPTER 13

DRINK THE CUP?

What does "Drink the cup" mean?

Please refer Matt. 26:39, Matt. 20:23. Here the reference is to the "cup".

"And he went a little further, and fell on his face, and prayed, saying, O my Father, if it be possible, let this cup pass from me: nevertheless not as I will, but as thou wilt" (Matthew 26:39)

"And he saith unto them, ye shall drink indeed of my cup, and be baptized with the baptism that I am baptized with: but to sit on my right hand, and on my left, is not mine to give, but it shall be given to them for whom it is prepared of my Father".
(Matthew 20:23)

Many have interpreted several times that we cannot drink "cup" because it is solid, therefore, obviously the reference is to the contents of the cup. Also, the verb "drink" means swallow liquid. Here, when Jesus said "let this cup pass from me", was He saying let the contents of this cup pass from me?

Some have said the contents were wine, some have said it is grape juice, and some have said it was plain water. However, we never come across any reference where it says that Jesus and His disciples drank 'wine' or 'grape juice', or plain water. Most reliable interpretation could be "fruit of the vine" as used in Mark 14:25

"Verily I say unto you, I will drink no more of the fruit of the vine, until that day that I drink it new in the kingdom of God". (Mark 14:25)

However, there are debates on this point as well. Would believers have Lord's Supper in the Kingdom as well? What exactly this 'fruit of the vine' is? The debate is not within the scope of this post.

2. I was also convinced that drinking from multiple cups is not wrong in view of the fact that we are remembering the death of Jesus by breaking bread and drinking cup (as Scriptures say) keeping in view of the symbolism that represent the two sacraments – the death of Jesus as sacrifice for us, and the baptism, which is declaration outwardly and boldly the death, burial and resurrection of believer (it is outward proclamation of salvation). The entire body of Christ is the Church, and not individual entities.

3. The belief "Transubstantiation" is from Roman Catholics, who say that in Eucharist the bread actually turns as the body of Jesus, and the wine actually turns into blood. That, I think is an error of understanding. Not even once in the Gospels, or in 1

Corinthians 10th and 11th chapters, the contents of the 'cup' were mentioned.

4. Luke 22:19 and 20 read…"And he took bread, and gave thanks, and brake it, and gave unto them, saying, this is my body which is given for you: this do in remembrance of me. Likewise also the cup after supper, saying, and this cup is the new testament in my blood, which is shed for you"

What this "Cup" actually refers to, is the wrath of God. It comes basically from the Old Testament and the New Testament corroborates it. Please read…

Jeremiah 25:15; Isaiah 51:17; Matt 20:20-28 and Revelation 14:9-10

"For thus saith the LORD God of Israel unto me; Take the wine cup of this fury at my hand, and cause all the nations, to whom I send thee, to drink it" (Jeremiah 25:15)

"Awake, awake, stand up, O Jerusalem, which hast drunk at the hand of the LORD the cup of his fury; thou hast drunken the dregs of the cup of trembling, and wrung them out" (Isaiah 51:17)

"And the third angel followed them, saying with a loud voice, If any man worship the beast and his image, and receive his mark in his forehead, or in his hand, The same shall drink of the wine

Leslie M John

of the wrath of God, which is poured out without mixture into the cup of his indignation; and he shall be tormented with fire and brimstone in the presence of the holy angels, and in the presence of the Lamb" (Revelation 14:9-10)

It is all about the wrath of God, and the Son of God, taking upon Himself that wrath, on behalf of mankind. Lord Jesus drank the 'CUP' on behalf of us, and we remember His sacrifice offered at the cross on behalf of us. This is the way not only for us to remember His death on the cross, but also to show to the world, of God's mercy, in bruising His only Son, who drank that cup for us.

CHAPTER 14

INCORRUPTIBLE INHERITANCE

"Blessed be the God and Father of our Lord Jesus Christ, who according to his abundant mercy has begotten us again unto a lively hope by the resurrection of Jesus Christ from the dead, to an inheritance incorruptible, and undefiled, and that fades not away, reserved in heaven for you" 1 Peter 1:3-4

Addressing the strangers throughout Pontus, Galatia, Cappadocia, Asia and Bithynia Peter, the disciple of Lord Jesus Christ calls on the "elect" by God the Father and wishes them "Grace".

The letter and the observations of Peter are applicable to all of us. Every believer in Christ is begotten unto the lively hope of eternal incorruptible inheritance, by the grace of God, and by the resurrection of Lord Jesus Christ from the dead.

The Lord defeated death when rose from the dead on the third day after His crucifixion. He was crucified on the cross even though He was declared innocent, and without any blemish. In His blood are our sins cleansed.

The promise of cleansing of our sins is made in the lives of everyone, who confesses that Jesus is Lord, and believes in

Leslie M John

heart that God raised Him from the dead on the third day. It is not the cleansing of our external body that perishes at our death, but it is the cleansing of our dead spirit that takes place when we invite Lord Jesus Christ into our lives.

Our body perishes at our death, and we will be given a glorified body at our resurrection. We will be conformed to the image of Lord Jesus Christ and be with Him forever and ever.

The inheritance promised to the children of God is undefiled and incorruptible. The rewards that are reserved for the believers in Christ, in heaven, do not fade away.

Our spirit that was dead in trespasses is quickened and made alive by Lord Jesus Christ the moment we accept Him as our personal savior. He lives in us.

"All scripture is given by inspiration of God, and is profitable for doctrine, for reproof, for correction, for instruction in righteousness" 2 Timothy 3:16

Every believer in Christ, irrespective of whether or not he is Jew or Gentile, is a New Man in Christ. It is inevitable that as long as we live on this earth we would face trials, tribulations, sickness etc. but that grate reward in heaven cannot be robbed from us by Satan, or anyone in this world. Thanks to God that we are born of the Spirit.

Great Commission and Spirit Soul and Body

"That which is born of the flesh is flesh; and that which is born of the Spirit is spirit" (John 3:6)

The power of God will keep us secure unto everlasting life in heaven, where there is no pain, or suffering, or death.

"And every man that strives for the mastery is temperate in all things. Now they do it to obtain a corruptible crown; but we an incorruptible". (1 Corinthians 9:25)

"In a moment, in the twinkling of an eye, at the last trump: for the trumpet shall sound, and the dead shall be raised incorruptible, and we shall be changed". (1 Corinthians 15:52)

"Being born again, not of corruptible seed, but of incorruptible, by the word of God, who lives and abides forever" (1 Peter 1:23)

Leslie M John

CHAPTER 15

JESUS SAVES

JESUS SAID "Except a man be born again, he cannot see the kingdom of God"

What does it mean to be born-again?

"Jesus answered and said unto him, Verily, verily, I say unto thee, Except a man be born again, he cannot see the kingdom of God. Nicodemus saith unto him, how can a man be born when he is old? Can he enter the second time into his mother's womb, and be born? Jesus answered, Verily, verily, I say unto thee, Except a man be born of water and of the Spirit, he cannot enter into the kingdom of God". (John 3:3-5)

Jesus Christ died for our sins; he rose from the dead and ascended into heaven. He is now seated at the right hand of the Majesty and He is coming again soon.

THIS IS HOW SIN CONQURED MAN

Holy Bible says God created man in his own image. God planted a garden eastward in Eden and he put there the man whom God called Adam.

The garden was indeed beautiful with every tree pleasant to sight and good for food. The LORD God made every tree to grow from the ground, the tree of life also in the midst of the garden, and the tree of knowledge of good and evil.

The LORD God put the man into the Garden of Eden to dress it and keep it. He said to the man that he may freely eat of every tree of the garden but of the tree of knowledge of good and evil he shall not eat; and in the day he eats it he shall surely die.

God saw that man was alone and the LORD God said that the man should not be alone. He decided to give a "help meet" for man.

The LORD God caused a deep sleep upon Adam and while he was sleeping God took one of the ribs of the man and made a woman out of the rib and brought to him. Adam called her as "Woman" because she was taken out of Man.

God said to the man to be fruitful, multiply, replenish the earth, and subdue it and have dominion over the fish of the sea, fowl of the air and every living thing that moves on the earth. (Genesis 2:8-28).

THIS IS HOW SATAN DECEIVED MAN

The serpent, who was more subtle than any other beast of the field, deceived the woman with his enticing words.

The serpent spoke to her and convinced her that God did not tell the truth. The woman yielded to the temptation of the serpent.

She saw that the tree was good for food and pleasure for the eyes and thought the tree would give her intelligence. She took of its fruit and ate and also gave to her husband and he ate it.

The eyes of both of them opened and they knew that they were naked. They made aprons for themselves with fig-leaves and when they heard the voice of God, whose name is "Jehovah Elohim" they hid themselves from his presence.

Jehovah Elohim called man and asked him where he was? The man said he feared because he was naked and hid himself.

God demanded an answer from the man as to who said to him that he was naked and questioned if he had he eaten fruit of the tree that he was asked not to eat from! The man blamed woman and the woman blamed the serpent.

THE CURSE FROM GOD FOLLOWED

The LORD God cursed the earth for man; the woman with pain in her child labor, and God cursed serpent that the serpent would crawl all the days of his life.

This resulted in Adam toiling for food; woman who was in Adam and who became his wife to be a help-mate was cursed with pain in her child-bearing.

The serpent who was not crawling before became a most loathed reptile on the earth to crawl on the earth his entire life. God put enmity between the seed of the woman and of the serpent.

Adam called the woman as "Eve" because she was the mother of all living. This is how the sin entered the world. In order to reconcile man to God, Jesus relinquished his glory in heaven and came down into this world in the form of man and lived among us.

"And I will put enmity between thee and the woman, and between thy seed and her seed; it shall bruise thy head, and thou shalt bruise his heel". (Genesis 3:15)

GOD SENT HIS ONLY BEGOTTEN SON FOR OUR SAKE

"For God so loved the world, that he gave his only begotten Son, that whosoever believeth in him should not perish, but have everlasting life" (John 3:16)

Jesus said: "Therefore doth my Father love me, because I lay down my life, that I might take it again". (John 10:17)

Leslie M John

SALVATION IS FREE OF COST

According to Bible good works alone will not get us into heaven but faith in Lord Jesus Christ alone saves us.

Confession by mouth and the belief that God raised Him from the dead will get us salvation free of cost. Salvation is free. No amount of good works can get a person a place in heaven.

The works will follow faith in Jesus Christ and salvation. May the Word of God speak to our hearts?

Heavenly Father's love is shown in John Chapter 3:16. He sent His only begotten Son, Jesus Christ for our sake that whosoever believes in him should not perish but have everlasting life. There is a clause which is conditional here.

The condition is that a person has to believe that The Father has sent His only begotten Son, Jesus Christ into this world for the remission of our sins. The purpose of sending Jesus into this world was that whoever believes in Him through Jesus Christ he will have everlasting life.

The initial mission of Jesus was to seek the lost sheep of Israel. Jesus also said to his twelve disciples not to go into the way of the Gentiles and into any city of Samaritans. This was the time when Jesus preached the Kingdom of heaven. (Matthew 10:5-6).

Great Commission and Spirit Soul and Body

Later in Mathew Chapter 15 we see that a Gentile woman from Canaan approached Jesus and prayed to him addressing him as "O Lord, thou Son of David" and crying out to have mercy on her because her daughter was grievously vexed with a devil.

Jesus did not answer her testing her faith but when his disciples interceded to send her away because she was crying, Jesus answered and said he was not sent but unto the lost sheep of the house of the Israel.

This should not be misunderstood that Jesus came into this world only for the sake of Jews.

It is indeed true that his first priority was to seek the lost sheep of Israel.

Until his crucifixion Jesus was under the Law of Moses. It was divine plan that Jesus should keep the Law of Moses meticulously; yet Jesus being the Son of God, had compassion on the Gentile woman that her faith was great and granted to her answer to her prayer and her daughter was made whole from that very hour. (Matthew 15:22-28).

Jesus nailed the handwritten laws and ordinances of Moses at the cross because they were contrary to the Gentiles. Those ordinances were blotted out as Apostle Paul wrote in Colossians 2:14.

Leslie M John

The message of Salvation is sent out to everyone on the earth after resurrection of Jesus Christ as per the commission given by Jesus in Matthew Chapter 28:19-20 and Acts 1:8

David wrote in Psalm 28:1 "Unto thee will I cry, O LORD my rock; be not silent to me: lest, if thou be silent to me, I become like them that go down into the pit" God will answer our prayers when we pray with faith.

In the Gospel according to John Chapter 10 God's love is shown toward all those who believe in him. There is a security of salvation assured.

Jesus is the Good Shepherd. Jesus said: "Therefore doth my Father love me, because I lay down my life, that I might take it again". (John 10:17).

The believer in Christ is not redeemed with corruptible things such as silver and gold or from vain conversations of forefathers but by the precious blood of Lord Jesus Christ. (1 Peter 1:18)

God had sent Jesus Christ to be a propitiation for us and whoever believes in him shall be redeemed of his sin and justified before him. (Romans 3:25, 1 John 2:2)

"Herein is love, not that we loved God, but that he loved us, and sent his Son to be the propitiation for our sins".1 John 4:10

"In whom we have redemption through his blood, the forgiveness of sins, according to the riches of his grace; Ephesians 1:7

"And that he might reconcile both unto God in one body by the cross, having slain the enmity thereby" Ephesians 2:16

"In whom we have redemption through his blood, even the forgiveness of sins: Colossians 1:14

"And, having made peace through the blood of his cross, by him to reconcile all things unto himself; by him, I say, whether they be things in earth, or things in heaven". Colossians 1:20

God loved us first and not that we did first. That is the reason why, though we trespassed His commandments, He sent His one and only Son, Jesus Christ to die on our stead.

JESUS CONQURED SATAN

"So Christ was once offered to bear the sins of many; and unto them that look for him shall he appear the second time without sin unto salvation". Hebrews 9:28

"That if thou shalt confess with thy mouth the Lord Jesus, and shalt believe in thine heart that God hath raised him from the dead, thou shalt be saved". Romans 10:9

"Whom God hath raised up, having loosed the pains of death: because it was not possible that he should be holden of it". (Acts 2:24)

"But ye shall receive power, after that the Holy Ghost is come upon you: and ye shall be witnesses unto me both in Jerusalem, and in all Judaea, and in Samaria, and unto the uttermost part of the earth. And when he had spoken these things, while they beheld, he was taken up; and a cloud received him out of their sight. And while they looked steadfastly toward heaven as he went up, behold, two men stood by them in white apparel; which also said, ye men of Galilee, why stand ye gazing up into heaven? This same Jesus, which is taken up from you into heaven, shall so come in like manner as ye have seen him go into heaven." (Acts 1:8-11)

Jesus died for our sake; he was buried, and was raised from the dead. Jesus, who is the seed of the woman crushed the head of the serpent at the cross.

Jesus rose from the dead on the third day and he appeared to many. Death could not hold him in the grave and He conquered death. Later after forty days he ascended into heaven. Jesus will come again in the same manner he ascended into heaven.

MESSAGE OF SALVATION

By offering Himself upon the cross of Calvary, Jesus opened the way for everyone to be saved. Jesus died for our sake as atonement for our sins. He was the perfect sacrifice. Jesus said "whosoever believeth in him should not perish, but have everlasting life".

Jesus, who is righteous, declares us righteous upon our confession of our sins. Through the blood of Jesus Christ we have the redemption and the forgiveness of our sins.

It pleased the Father to bruise him for sake and He did that according to his riches in Grace. Grace alone saves us. We are redeemed from our sins and have obtained forgiveness of our sins through Jesus Christ.

Jesus died upon the cross of Calvary so that we may be reconciled unto Him. There is no difference whether we are Jews or Gentiles we are all one in Christ.

Jesus died for all of us, and he rose from the dead and ascended in to heaven. We, who were His enemies, are made His children.

The opposition that was caused between God and Man by man's sin is reconciled once and for all by Jesus Christ dying on the cross for our sake. We are reconciled unto God through His

Leslie M John

blood that was shed upon the cross of Calvary. All that we have to do is to believe that Jesus is the Lord.

INVITATION TO SALVATION

Today is the day of Salvation. It is your choice. Jesus Christ, who bore our sins and died for our sake, is resurrected and He is living God. He will come soon to receive the saved ones to be with Him eternally.

Please do not lose this opportunity but confess your sins to him and be saved. It is not a way to convert you Christianity. God has his own ways of gaining men for himself. My message is a request that you may please accept Jesus Christ as your personal Savior, and as your Lord, so that you may have everlasting life just as I have gained peace through Him

CHAPTER 16

WHY HAVE YOU FORSAKEN ME?

Eli, Eli, lama sabachthani?

(My God, my God, why hast thou forsaken me?)

From Matthew 27:46

"Now from the sixth hour there was darkness over all the land unto the ninth hour. And about the ninth hour Jesus cried with a loud voice, saying, Eli, Eli, lama sabachthani? that is to say, My God, my God, why hast thou forsaken me?" (Matthew 27:45-46)

From the sixth hour of the day in Jerusalem until the ninth of hour there, which is equivalent to 12.00 PM to 3.00 PM of our time, there was utter darkness on the face of the earth when Jesus was on the cross, bearing our sin upon Himself.

It pleased the Father to bruise His Son Jesus for our sin (cf. prophecy in Isaiah 53:10), and our sin was judged at the cross by the righteous Lord God.

"Yet it pleased the LORD to bruise him; he hath put him to grief: when thou shalt make his soul an offering for sin, he shall see his seed, he shall prolong his days, and the pleasure of the LORD shall prosper in his hand" (Isaiah 53:10)

109

Leslie M John

It was at that time that the Father brought about severest darkness on the face of the earth. Jesus took our punishment on Himself and our sin on Him was judged at the Cross.

The Father, the Holy One, could not see the sin on the Son Jesus Christ, and that is the reason why the Father judged the sin at the cross where Lord Jesus was hung bearing our sin. Darkness signifies judgment and during this darkness our sin was judged at the Cross.

"For he hath made him to be sin for us, who knew no sin; that we might be made the righteousness of God in him" (2 Corinthians 5:21)

"Christ hath redeemed us from the curse of the law, being made a curse for us: for it is written, Cursed is every one that hangeth on a tree" (Galatians 3:13)

"His body shall not remain all night on the tree, but you shall bury him the same day, for a hanged man is cursed by God. You shall not defile your land that the LORD your God is giving you for an inheritance" (Deuteronomy 21:23 ESV)

Jesus, who knew no sin, was made sin for us in order that we might be made the righteousness of God in Him.

There are contentious beliefs that Father can look upon the sin of man, and therefore, Jesus was not forsaken; but considering the fact that sin is pernicious, heinous, offensive and polluted, it is hardly believable that the Holy Father God could see sin upon the Son of God.

In the Old Testament according to the Law, Moses was commanded by the LORD, to burn the bullock, and his hide, his flesh and his dung outside the camp.

This shadow was fulfilled in Jesus when the sin on Him was judged at Golgotha, outside the city, in order that He may become propitiation and die a substitutionary death on behalf of us to redeem us to give us everlasting life. Anyone can receive this everlasting life by believing that Jesus is the Lord and God raised Him from the dead.

"But the bullock, and his hide, his flesh, and his dung, he burnt with fire without the camp; as the LORD commanded Moses" (Leviticus 8:17)

It was neither an eclipse nor was the usual darkness that came at sunset, but it was utter darkness from noon to three past noon. It was during the Passover that this darkness came upon the face of the earth and this darkness prevailed on the face of the earth in the midst of the day light. It was indeed unusual.

"Verily, verily, I say unto you, He that heareth my word, and believeth on him that sent me, hath everlasting life, and shall

Leslie M John

not come into condemnation; but is passed from death unto life". (John 5:24)

Darkness was one of the ten plagues that God brought on Egypt. "And the LORD said unto Moses, Stretch out thine hand toward heaven, that there may be darkness over the land of Egypt, even darkness [which] may be felt. And Moses stretched forth his hand toward heaven; and there was a thick darkness in all the land of Egypt three days" Exodus 10:21, 22

"And it came between the camp of the Egyptians and the camp of Israel; and it was a cloud and darkness to them, but it gave light by night to these: so that the one came not near the other all the night". (Exodus 14:20)

Darkness is accompanied with fear, sin, and judgment. It is opposed to luster and honor. It is opposed to wisdom; it is associated with confusion, folly, vexation of Spirit, and calamities.

An angel shone light towards Israelites when Israelites were just about to cross Red Sea, and darkness to Pharaoh and his army.

It was the judgment that Pharaoh and his army were about to face while the children of God were about to cross the Red Sea.

Great Commission and Spirit Soul and Body

Scriptures speak of the sun and the moon getting fully darkened, and the stars withdrawing their shining in the last days. It happens when the Lord comes again to this earth.

"The sun and the moon shall be darkened, and the stars shall withdraw their shining". (Joel 3:15)

When Jesus was on the cross he quoted directly from Psalm 22:1 and cried aloud "Eli, Eli, lama sabachthani? That is to say, My God, my God, why hast thou forsaken me?"

"My God, my God, why hast thou forsaken me? Why art thou so far from helping me, and from the words of my roaring?" (Psalms 22:1)

Although the details of separation or non-separation of the Father and the Son at the cross, for a while, are known to the Father and the Son only, yet it is worth considering, to the best of our knowledge, whether or not the Son was forsaken at the Lord's death and why Lord Jesus said "My God, my God, why hast thou forsaken me?"

It is necessary that we understand what exactly happened during those dark hours, and the way the Father judged sin upon the Son.

Lord Jesus had two natures in His incarnation when He relinquished His glory that He had with the Father and came

113

into this world in the form of a servant and in the likeness of man.

One nature that He had was of divine and the other of human. He felt the human traits such as joy, pain, sadness, hunger. He wept at the tomb of Lazarus, who was dead for four days.

However, the pain He suffered at the cross was, indeed, much more in its intensity. He bore our sin and took the penalty of our sin upon Himself and paid for our sin and punishment.

It was not by silver or by gold that we were redeemed but by His precious blood, and therefore, the cost of our redemption was very heavy.

Lord Jesus felt separation from the Father just as the David felt separation from God but the Lord was not forsaken to be our savior or ceased to be God. He was for a short while, in His human nature, felt all alone while our sin was on Him.

God is Almighty, who is triune, and who lives forever and ever, is inseparable. God is omnipresent, omniscient, and omnipotent.

"Thus saith the LORD, The heaven is my throne, and the earth is my footstool: where is the house that ye build unto me? And where is the place of my rest?" (Isaiah 66:1)

It would also be apt to consider here whether or not David felt separation from God when He cried "My God, my God, why hast thou forsaken me? Why art thou so far from helping me, and from the words of my roaring?" (Psalms 22:1)

The caption of the Psalm is "To the chief Musician upon Aijeleth Shahar, A Psalm of David" David was singing a song extemporarily, an unknown tune, pointing to Lord Jesus Christ's sufferings than to himself.

It was an unknown future to him. When He sang the song He neither felt Jesus would be separated from the Father or not but He said "My God, my God why hast thou forsaken me" in prophecy.

The psalm is Messianic. He did not mean Jesus would be separated or would not be separated; however the word meaning of "forsaken" is abandon.

David lost fellowship with God when He had illegal relationship with Bathsheba and got her husband Uriah killed. His sin did not go unpunished. God dealt with Him severely but taking away his firstborn son, and putting him to terrible ignominy (Ref. 2 Samuel 12:1-19).

Similarly when Jesus was on the cross He, in His human nature was bearing our sin and that sin was judged severely by the Father and Jesus felt separation from the Father; however God

115

raised Him from the dead and said to Him "You are my Son, today I have begotten you".

So also Christ did not exalt himself to be made a high priest, but was appointed by him who said to him, "You are my Son, today I have begotten you"; (Hebrews 5:5 ESV)

Psalmist goes on singing the song indicating the Lord's exaltation in His future kingdom. He concludes the psalm in praises and the Lord's exaltation as the King.

"All the prosperous of the earth eat and worship; before him shall bow all who go down to the dust, even the one who could not keep himself alive. Posterity shall serve him; it shall be told of the Lord to the coming generation; they shall come and proclaim his righteousness to a people yet unborn, that he has done it" (Psalm 22:29-31 ESV)

Lord Jesus said:

"I and my Father are one". (John 10:30)

Although the word "forsaken" in Hebrew, Greek and in English means "abandon" Lord Jesus Christ was not forsaken eternally, but He felt separation from the Father, because He was bearing our sin upon Himself, and that is why He was quoting from Psalm 22:1 when He cried "My God, my God, why hast thou forsaken me?"

Great Commission and Spirit Soul and Body

Great Commission and Spirit Soul and Body

"And about the ninth hour Jesus cried with a loud voice, saying, Eli, Eli, lama sabachthani? That is to say, My God, my God, why hast thou forsaken me?" (Matthew 27:46)

Let us worship the Father in the name of our Lord and Savior Jesus Christ, who was crucified, died for our sake, was buried and was raised from the dead on the third day. Jesus ascended into heaven and he is seated on the right hand of the Majesty.

CHAPTER 17

REDEEMED FROM BONDAGE OF SIN

"So also is the resurrection of the dead. It is sown in corruption; it is raised in incorruption" (1 Corinthians 15:42)

Bible says we were dead in trespasses and sins; but to those who believed in Jesus Christ as personal savior, it is the quickening of the spirit.

We, who are born again, are redeemed from the bondage of sin. We are saved unto eternal life.

Sin held us as slaves; made us blind to the truth of the Gospel of Jesus Christ; made us liable for condemnation; had us as aliens from the commonwealth of Israel; strangers to the covenants of promise; had us in a state of hopelessness, and it treated us a strangers and foreigners to the living God.

However, God delivered us and made us servants of righteousness. We, who were the children of wrath are given the privilege of calling the living God, as 'Abba, Father'. He has given us the privilege of be called as sons of God. He has translated us into the Kingdom of His dear Son.

Dead in trespasses does not mean that a man is fully dead in all respects to the extent that he can not believe on Jesus, but it means that Satan has blinded his belief and understanding to the extent that the Scriptural truth appears to him as foolishness. (Ref: Eph 2nd Chapter, 2 Cor. 4:3-4, Romans 6:17-18, John 3:19-20, Mark 2:17, Luke 15th Chapter, Col 1:13)

The only requirement that God has placed on a sinner is to repent of his sins and call on Jesus to forgive his/her sins. Entire price for redemption from sinful life is paid for by Jesus on the cross.

There is nothing that a sinner needs to do except believing in the blood of Jesus, who paid the price for our redemption already.

God formed our bodies with the dust of the ground. When he created the first man, on this earth he breathed his life into the nostrils of the man and the man (Adam) became a living soul.

The living soul that God created was in the image of God.

After man had committed sin he lost that image of God, and 'death reigned from Adam to Moses even over that had not sinned after the similitude of Adam's transgression'.

By the offence of one many came under the penalty of death, but by the gift of God that is 'grace' many have become eligible to receive eternal life.

Leslie M John

It was by one, (Adam), who sinned that death came to reign on man, and it is by the ONE (Jesus), that the gift of God is available for all sinners.

All those who accept that the Son of God, Jesus, died for his/her sins, and accept him as the 'Lord' of one's life are saved from damnation.

It is then that the soul dead in trespasses is redeemed; it is then that the soul is delivered from suffering the wrath of God. The soul that does not repent of his/her sins will be cast into lake of fire, by God, after the 'Great white throne judgment', which is the final judgment.

As and when our earthly house of this tabernacle gets dissolved we gain a building of God, the house not made with hands, but that which would be eternal in heaven.

We groan in this body desiring to be clothed upon with the house that we would have in heavens, and that glorified body, which resurrects from the dead, when Jesus comes again, would not be naked; but the living soul with eternal life that does not marry nor is given in marriage. (Ref: 2 Corinthians. 5th Chapter of Matthew22:30 and Romans 5th Chapter.)

Apostle Peter reveals a marvelous truth in 1 Peter 1st Chapter. Addressing to the strangers scattered throughout Pontus, Galatia, Cappadocia, Asia and Bithynia he calls on Elect by God the Father, and wishes them 'Grace'. All those, whom he addressed were, as he says, were begotten unto lively hope by the resurrection of Jesus Christ from the dead and to inherit incorruptible, and undefiled rewards that do not fade away. These are reserved for them in heaven.

If we read 2 Timothy 3:16 it says, 'All scripture is given by inspiration of God, and is profitable for doctrine, for reproof, for correction, for instruction in righteousness'.

Depending upon 2 Timothy 3:16 every one, irrespective of his belonging to the clan of Jews or Gentiles can claim this verse to be applicable in one's life, provided he/she has accepted Jesus Christ as his/her personal Savior.

The power of God keeps us and assures us that inheritance, which is in heaven. We have the eternal life to be with the Lord Jesus Christ always. That inheritance is incorruptible, and undefiled. It does not fade away. We may face trials and tribulations in this world, but the rewards that are reserved for us in eternity are great and beyond description.

If we call on the Father, He will help us to pass our pilgrimage on this earth in fear of Him, rendering to Him His due worship. We are not redeemed by silver or gold, but by the blood of His only begotten Son Jesus Christ, whom John identified as the Lamb of God. Peter confirms that this Lamb of God was Lord

Jesus. John said this is the Lamb of God came to this world to take away the sin of the world.

The Father in heaven judges every man according to his/her works while sojourning on this earth. He keeps record of our vain conversations that we may have received from our earthly fathers following traditions.

Therefore, let us keep in mind that as the Scripture says, Lord Jesus Christ was 'foreordained before the foundation of the world' and he was revealed unto us in the form of man. He died on the cross, bearing our sins, so that we may have redemption from sin. God raised him from the dead on the third day after crucifixion.

Jesus is not dead lying in the grave just as any other man; but he was raised from the dead on the third day as prophesied. Later, after forty days on this earth he ascended into heaven. He is now seated on the right hand of the Majesty, pleading on our behalf with the Father. Our faith in God increases as our days pass on this earth because of this infallible truth.

Our souls are purified by believing on this truth and hope increases as our sojourning on this earth tapers to start afresh eternal life with the only one, who paid the price for our salvation. Likewise, our love for one another should be fervent and pure. Just as grass withers, and flower fades, our life on this earth is also temporal and temporary, but the life with Jesus is eternal as the Word of God endures for ever. (I Peter 1st Chapter)

Apostle Paul warned (in Romans 1st Chapter) all those Romans that they had changed the glory of the un-corruptible God into images of God's creation. They made beasts and creeping things and made them as their own gods. Therefore, 'God also gave them up to uncleanness through the lusts of their own hearts to dishonor their own bodies between themselves'.

But for those, who honor Lord Jesus Christ and take refuge in him, there is hope that they will rise from the dead unto incorruption. The body of the believer in Christ is raised in power, even though on this earth he/she was in weakness. The believer in Christ rises in an incorruptible body that has natural body and also spiritual body. The first man Adam was made a living soul and the last Adam (Jesus) was made a quickening spirit. 1 Corinthians 15:42-45

It is a great blessing because we, who were dead in trespasses and sins, are also quickened.

"And you hath he quickened, who were dead in trespasses and sins" **Ephesians 2:1**"

Leslie M John

CHAPTER 18

REPENTENCE AND CHRISTIANITY

It is interesting to note that Lord Jesus never said about conversion from one's religion to Christianity; but rather what He said was to "Repent". In the normal course of reading Bible we do not need to consider how a certain word was used in the original language, but when it becomes contentious, it is necessary that we search the actual meaning of that word used in a given context, and it is imperative that we understand correctly as to how the said word was used in the language in which it was originally written.

The title "Christians" for the followers of Christ has come into existence much later after Jesus died and rose from the dead, and ascended into heaven.

The title "Christians" was given in derision by the enemies of followers of Christ, as some believe. Reading through Acts chapter 11 would give good idea as to why the followers of Christ were called "Christians".

"And when he had found him, he brought him unto Antioch. And it came to pass, that a whole year they assembled themselves with the church, and taught much people. And the disciples were called Christians first in Antioch" (Acts 11:26)

"Yet if any man suffer as a Christian, let him not be ashamed; but let him glorify God on this behalf" (1 Peter 4:16)

FEW LINES FROM HISTORY

King Saul, King David and King Solomon ruled whole of Israel, but King Saul's ways were not pleasing to God, and, therefore, the LORD gave the reign to King David, who was successful for many years, but on one point he failed. He counted his army as if to show that he was winning wars by his own power. In fact, he won all his wars with the help and leadership of God.

When it was time for David's son, Solomon to take over the reign the LORD gave him David's throne and said to him to keep the LORD's commandments and statutes.

King Solomon, however, disobeyed God and married wives from heathen, who led him to worship idols. His disobedience resulted in God's wrath coming upon him. God split his kingdom into two; giving northern kingdom to Jeroboam, and the southern kingdom to Rehoboam.

Nineteen kings ruled northern kingdom in succession, and twenty kings ruled southern kingdom in succession. Thereafter, Babylonians under the leadership of Nebuchadnezzar took over Southern Kingdom, and Assyrians took over Northern Kingdom. Finally Babylonians humbled Assyrians, and the history is huge thereafter.

Leslie M John

When Jesus came into this world, His initial mission was to the Jews, and then to the Gentiles. He said

"...Repent ye: for the kingdom of heaven is at hand" (Matthew 3:2)

He was in fact saying to them, the united kingdom of Israel was soon to come, and they should change their understanding about Jesus, who repeatedly said to them He came from the Father, making it clear that He was the Messiah.

However, Jews rejected Him as Messiah, which resulted in postponing uniting Northern Kingdom and Southern Kingdom and making them one. Jews expected Messiah to come like a king and like a warrior and defeat opposing forces, and establish earthly kingdom uniting Northern Kingdom and Southern Kingdom.

However, the Lord came into this world in a humble way. He relinquished His glory with the Father, and incarnated in the form of a servant and in the likeness of man. He was born of Virgin Mary, when the Holy Spirit came upon her and the power of the High overshadowed her.

Therefore, He was called the "Son of God". Mary wrapped Him in swaddling clothes, and laid in a manger because there was no room for them in the inn (cf. Luke 1:35; Luke 2:7)

Great Commission and Spirit Soul and Body

Great Commission and Spirit Soul and Body

The Lord's second coming of Lord Jesus Christ is imminent. The Lord will "descend from heaven with a shout, with the voice of the archangel, and with the trump of God: and the dead in Christ shall rise first: Then we which are alive and remain shall be caught up together with them in the clouds, to meet the Lord in the air: and so shall we ever be with the Lord" (1 Thessalonians 4:16-17)

"In a moment, in the twinkling of an eye, at the last trump: for the trumpet shall sound, and the dead shall be raised incorruptible, and we shall be changed" (1 Corinthians 15:52)

After the Lord makes His second appearance on this earth, He will literally rule for thousand years from the throne of David in due course of time. The prophecies will literally be fulfilled.

People who saw Jesus perform miracles were in hurry to make Him King, rather than wait for the Lord's time. They were impressed by His ministry.

Therefore, at one point of time they tried to take Jesus by force and make Him King over Israel, but the Lord refused such invitation, and left them. His hour had not come. He will be King of kings, and Lord of lords surely when the Father enforces His time upon men.

"Then those men, when they had seen the miracle that Jesus did, said, This is of a truth that prophet that should come into

Leslie M John

the world. When Jesus therefore perceived that they would come and take him by force, to make him a king, he departed again into a mountain himself alone" (John 6:14-15)

At the end of His mission, when the Lord was under trial before Pilate, He said His kingdom was not of this world, indicating that His kingdom is of Spiritual kingdom.

"Jesus answered, "My kingdom is not of this world. If my kingdom were of this world, my servants would have been fighting, that I might not be delivered over to the Jews. But my kingdom is not from the world." Then Pilate said to him, "So you are a king?"

Jesus answered, "You say that I am a king. For this purpose I was born and for this purpose I have come into the world—to bear witness to the truth. Everyone who is of the truth listens to my voice." (John 18:36, 37 ESV)

REPENTANCE:

Here, considering how the word "Repent" came into be used, in the context where it was used, it can be seen that the word was translated from the word "metanoeo" from Greek Strong's word 3340 "metanoeo". It means "to think differently or afterwards, i.e. reconsider (morally, feel compunction); not to miss the mark; not transgressing the law".

Great Commission and Spirit Soul and Body

Hebrew Strong's number: 2398. chata' which means not to miss; it is same as the meaning of 'sin' is. That is not to miss the mark; not transgressing of the law.

Repentance, therefore, is the expression of true sorrow exercised towards God. It is not earning salvation by doing good works. Salvation is by grace through faith and by faith in Jesus Christ alone. It is the confession one makes of his one's sin committed against the Holy God, and eventually turning away from it altogether. In the context of New Testament it is change one's mind, especially toward Lord Jesus Christ (cf. Luke 3:8-14; Acts 3:19; Acts 26:20).

It is not like a prisoner feeling sorrow after committing a crime. Prisoner might feel sorrow and yet may not change his behavior and attitude; but it is the true sorrow exercised towards the Holy God, and changing altogether his behavior, attitude and life style.

Repentance is just as King David said in his Psalm 51:4.

"Against you, you only, have I sinned and done what is evil in your sight, so that you may be justified in your words and blameless in your judgment" (Psalm 51:4 ESV)

Apostle Paul describes true repentance in 2 Corinthians 7:10 that leads man to salvation; change one's mind that results in abstinence of sinning anymore. He also describes the sorrow of

Leslie M John

the world that leads to one's death, which consequently leads into the 'lake of fire', where gnashing of teeth does not cease and thirst that never quenches.

"For godly grief produces a repentance that leads to salvation without regret, whereas worldly grief produces death" (2 Corinthians 7:10 ESV)

The following are few references where Greek word "metanoeo" was used in the New Testament, and the corresponding Hebrew word Strong's number 2398 " chata" used in the Old Testament to emphasize on "to think differently or afterwards, i.e. reconsider (morally, feel compunction)"

References: Mt 3:2; 4:17; Mr 1:15; 6:12; Lu 13:3,5; 16:30; 17:3-4; Ac 2:38; 3:19; 8:22; 17:30; 26:20; 2Co 7:8; Heb 7:21; Re 2:5,16,21-22; 3:3,19

WHAT DID JESUS MEAN WHEN HE SAID "REPENT"?

Lord Jesus said

"...Repent ye: for the kingdom of heaven is at hand" (Matthew 3:2)

"And saying, The time is fulfilled, and the kingdom of God is at hand: repent ye, and believe the gospel" (Mark 1:15)

"And they went out, and preached that men should repent" (Mark 6:12)

Great Commission and Spirit Soul and Body

Great Commission and Spirit Soul and Body

"And that repentance and remission of sins should be preached in his name among all nations, beginning at Jerusalem" (Luke 24:47)

Some theologians think that the phrases "kingdom of heaven", "kingdom of Christ", and the "kingdom of God" refer to different kingdoms, mostly differentiating between "thousand year reign of Lord Jesus" and eternity; but in fact they all refer to one and only "kingdom of God" as we read in Daniel 7:13-14

"I saw in the night visions, and, behold, one like the Son of man came with the clouds of heaven, and came to the Ancient of days, and they brought him near before him. And there was given him dominion, and glory, and a kingdom, that all people, nations, and languages, should serve him: his dominion is an everlasting dominion, which shall not pass away, and his kingdom that which shall not be destroyed" (Daniel 7:13-14)

Peter, the disciple of Jesus said..."Repent ye therefore, and be converted, that your sins may be blotted out, when the times of refreshing shall come from the presence of the Lord" (Acts 3:19)

Sin leads a man to be cast into eternal hell, into "lake of fire" to be precise; but the gift of God is everlasting life.

When Apostle Paul was facing a trial he as a part of his defense he questioned King Agrippa if he believed in Prophets. Replying

Leslie M John

quickly to this, King Agrippa said "In a short time would you persuade me to be a Christian?"

"vs. 27 King Agrippa, do you believe the prophets? I know that you believe." vs. 28 And Agrippa said to Paul, "In a short time would you persuade me to be a Christian?" Acts 26:27.28

It is interesting conversation. Let us read this passage as it is in the Bible...

Vs. 24 And as he was saying these things in his defense, Festus said with a loud voice, "Paul, you are out of your mind; your great learning is driving you out of your mind."

Vs. 25 But Paul said, "I am not out of my mind, most excellent Festus, but I am speaking true and rational words.

Vs. 26 For the king knows about these things, and to him I speak boldly. For I am persuaded that none of these things has escaped his notice, for this has not been done in a corner.

Vs. 27 King Agrippa, do you believe the prophets? I know that you believe."

Vs. 28 And Agrippa said to Paul, "In a short time would you persuade me to be a Christian?"

Vs. 29 And Paul said, "Whether short or long, I would to God that not only you but also all who hear me this day might become such as I am—except for these chains." Acts 26:24-29 (ESV)

As Apostle Paul was giving his testimony, Festus accuses Paul saying he is out his mind because of his great learning, but Paul says he was not out of his mind, and was speaking the truth. In the meanwhile, Paul quickly turns to King Agrippa and appreciates King saying the happenings in those days did not escape king's notice, and the kind was not sitting in a corner either!

After hearing from King Agrippa Paul wished if King and all the people there hear him and become the followers of Lord Jesus Christ. It is worth appreciating Paul's boldness in preaching Gospel even while he was in bonds and facing trial.

The title "Christian" may be important, but what is more important is to become a follower of true teachings of Lord Jesus Christ to be surely blessed and to receive everlasting life.

It is not just following the teachings of the Lord, but accepting him into your life as your personal savior, because there is none, who died to save mankind from perishing unto everlasting life, and there is none, except Jesus Christ, who was raised by God unto everlasting life.

We will also die one day; however, all those who believe in Him will be raised from the dead, conformed to His image and live

133

with Him forever and ever. Others will be condemned and judged at the 'great white throne'. When they are judged as having transgressed the law of God, they will be cast into the 'lake of fire'.

"...if you confess with your mouth that Jesus is Lord and believe in your heart that God raised him from the dead, you will be saved. 10 For with the heart one believes and is justified, and with the mouth one confesses and is saved" (Romans 10:9-10 ESV)

CHAPTER 19

REWARDS FROM RIGHTEOUS JUDGE

"I have fought a good fight, I have finished my course, I have kept the faith" (2 Timothy 4:7)

At the fag-end of Paul's life when he knew that he would not live anymore, because of his impending execution unto death by Nero for preaching the Gospel, he writes letter to Timothy, whom he called as his son in faith and in Christian ministry, exhorting him to preach the word of God. He recollects his own ministry and says that he fought a good fight, finished his course, and kept the faith.

Paul, therefore, says that the Lord Jesus Christ will give him a crown of righteousness at the Judgment seat of Christ. He says not only he receives such crown of righteousness but all those who believe in Lord Jesus Christ and love His second coming.

"Henceforth there is laid up for me a crown of righteousness, which the Lord, the righteous judge, shall give me at that day: and not to me only, but unto all them also that love his appearing" (2 Timothy 4:8)

Bible speaks of five crowns and they are:

1. And every man that strives for the mastery is temperate in all things. Now they do it to obtain a corruptible crown; but we an incorruptible. (1 Corinthians 9:25)
2. For what is our hope, or joy, or crown of rejoicing? Are not even ye in the presence of our Lord Jesus Christ at his coming? (1 Thessalonians 2:19)
3. Henceforth there is laid up for me a crown of righteousness, which the Lord, the righteous judge, shall give me at that day: and not to me only, but unto all them also that love his appearing. (2 Timothy 4:8)
4. Blessed is the man that endureth temptation: for when he is tried, he shall receive the crown of life, which the Lord hath promised to them that love him. (James 1:12)
5. And when the chief Shepherd shall appear, ye shall receive a crown of glory that fades not away. (1 Peter 5:4)

Indeed, Paul struggled hard to proclaim the Gospel of Lord Jesus Christ from the beginning of his ministry. He had a bad past record of persecuting Christians. His name was Saul before his conversion to Christianity. He had consented to the death of Spirit-filled Stephen and kept the raiment of them that slew him. He threatened to slaughter the disciples of the Lord. He desired letters from high priest to Damascus to the synagogues that if he found any disciples of the Lord, whether be men or women, he would bring them bound to Jerusalem.

However, as he journeyed to Damascus he encountered Lord Jesus Christ on the way. There shone a great light suddenly from heaven around him. Saul fell down to the ground and he heard a voice asking him "Saul, Saul, why persecutest thou me?" Saul answered and said "Who are thou Lord?" Then the Lord answered him and said "I am Jesus whom thou persecute: it is hard for thee to kick against pricks".

It is indeed hard to be obstructive, or stubborn not to believe Jesus as the Lord and fight against His teachings. The ox that kicks against pricks hurts itself and none else. The pricks refereed to here are goads that the farmer uses to prick the ox while farming. The stubborn ox that kicks against such goads, which are sharp iron pieces stuck into the edge of the stick, injures itself and none else.

The Lord was using this phrase against Saul who was persecuting Christians and the disciples. Hurting Christians was like hurting Lord Jesus Christ Himself. Saul was thrown onto the ground and humbled in no time and was made blind. The voice from Lord Jesus Christ was heard by others who were accompanying Saul but they could not see any man. Saul humbled himself immediately.

It is the obedience and change of heart that God demands at a man's conversion to follow Jesus. Then there should be the willingness to accept Lord Jesus Christ as savior. Confessing by mouth the Lord Jesus Christ and believing in heart that God raised Him from the dead will earn salvation and that is called

Leslie M John

'born-again'. The salvation is neither earned by gold nor silver or good works but by faith in Him alone.

"That if thou shalt confess with thy mouth the Lord Jesus, and shalt believe in thine heart that God hath raised him from the dead, thou shalt be saved" (Romans 10:9).